Virgin Mary as the Lioness of Judah

The Generations of God-carriers

© 2024 Copyright Author, Anthony Mofunanya

All rights reserved. No part of this publication may be reproduced, stored in a retrieval system, or transmitted, in any form or by any means, electronic, mechanical, photocopying, recording, or otherwise, without the written prior permission of the author.

The scripture references and citations are taken from the Jerusalem Bible, King James Version, New King James Version, New International Standard Version, and Amplified Bible. Emphasis, adaptations, and variances are the author's.

Bulk Purchase
To purchase in bulk with a discount for free distribution or to sponsor the free distribution of any number, you can contact the author via email: giftglobalinv@gmail.com

Prophet Habakkuk prophesied about the knowledge of God on earth thus: "For the earth shall be filled with the knowledge of the glory of the Lord, as the waters cover the sea" – Habakkuk 2:14. **Let us join hands together in spreading and saturating the earth with the knowledge of the Glory of the Lord!**

Email: giftglobalinv@gmail.com
Twitter: @GiftGlobaluk

Facebook: @Giftglobaluk

Instagram: @GiftGlobaluk

TikTok: @anthonymofunanya

PayPal: tonio4jm@outlook.com

© Copyright Author, Anthony Mofunanya
ISBN:

Publisher: Gift Global Ltd, London, UK

Dedication

Dedicatedly consecrated to Mary, **the Lioness of Judah**, the Mother of the Lion of Judah, the Mother of God whose soul a sword pierced as it pierced the soul of Jesus Christ. Dedicated also to all who acknowledge Her as their Mother.

Dedicated to all Her children that the Spirit spoke about in Revelation 12:17 thus: "Then the dragon was enraged at the woman and went off to wage war against the rest of her offspring—those who keep God's commands and hold fast their testimony about Jesus."

"The Lion of Judah was born by the Lioness of Judah. The Lion loudly roars! Never undermine the roaring of the Lioness no matter how discreet it sounds. She is a hunter! She is the mother of the Lion of Judah! She deserves to be honoured! She mirrors the dignity of womanhood." – The author.

"How can you ignore this woman that the sword which pierced the soul of Jesus Christ pierced her soul too? How can you not honour and respect such a woman? Remember, she was singularly honoured and highly favoured by the Almighty Father." – The author.

"The predestination of the Blessed Virgin as Mother of God was associated with the incarnation of the divine word: in the designs of divine Providence, she was the gracious mother of the divine Redeemer here on earth, and above all others and in a singular way the generous associate and humble handmaid of the Lord. She conceived, brought forth, and nourished Christ, she presented him to the Father in the temple, and shared her Son's sufferings as he died on the cross. Thus, in a wholly singular way, she cooperated by her obedience, faith, hope and burning charity in the work of the Saviour in restoring supernatural life to souls. **For this reason, she is a mother to us in the order of grace.**"

- Council Vatican II (Dogmatic constitution Lumen Gentium, 61-62, emphasis is mine)

Oh, how much humans bemoan the fall of the human race through Eve and Adam and speak against Eve for consenting to the seduction of Satan. Yet, how little we rejoice in our new creation through the Virgin Mary, the Lioness of Judah by the Holy Spirit in Jesus Christ! Oh, how it is that the entire humankind is supposed to exult and honour this Woman through whom we received the Saviour?

The scripture revealed: "Therefore if anyone is in Christ [that is, grafted in, joined to Him by faith in Him as Savior], **he is a new creature** [reborn and renewed by the Holy Spirit]; the old things [the previous moral and spiritual condition] have passed away. Behold, new things have come [because spiritual awakening brings a new life]." – 2 Corinthians 5:17 (AMP – emphasis is mine).

Table of Contents

Dedication 3
Table of Contents 1
Introduction 3
Prologue 6
Jesus Christ Is the Lion of Judah 8
The Lioness of Judah 10
The Virgin Mary Is the Lioness of Judah 13
The Biogenesis Law and the Lioness of Judah 16
The Lioness Character in Cana 19
The Lioness Character at Calvary 22
Jesus' Respect for His Mother 24
Be Imitators of the Lion of Judah 26
Mothers and Wives of Men and Women of God We Honour ... 28
Lioness of Judah and the Holy Land of Israel 30
Mary's Intercession and Intervention 32
Statues and Images of Mary the Lioness of Judah 35
Lioness of Judah in Catholicism and Pentecostalism 36
The Lioness Gave Birth to the Lion of Judah 38
The Lioness at Sacrificial Death of the Lion 41
Behold Lioness Prior and On the Pentecost Day 42
The Apostle John Took Mary Home 44
Mary's Influence on God's Kairos (Timing) 47
Privileged to be Visited by the Lioness of Judah 49

The Lioness of Judah is the Mother of Christians	51
Mary is the Lioness and the Sheep	56
Honour and Respect God's Choice	58
The Power of the Roaring Voice of the Lioness	61
Lioness of Judah Spoke in Tongues	63
The Mirror of the Divine Plan	65
Theotokos the Mother of the Lion of Judah	69
Inseparable Union of Jesus and Mary	73
Mary Must Respond for the Word to Incarnate	76
Imitate Mary in Response and Declaration of the Word	79
Mary's Knowledge of Jesus Christ	83
Mary and the Manifestation of the Invisible God	88
Glorification and Coronation of the Lioness of Judah	90
Thoughts of the Pope and Early Church Writers on Lioness of Judah	94
The Church's Early Writers on Mary	95
Exhortation – Wonderfully and Fearfully Made	98
How To Pray the Rosary	102

Introduction

The author, Anthony Mofunanya, in *The Virgin Mary as the Lioness of Judah: The Generations of God-carriers* reflects on the honour, favour, dignity and blessedness bestowed on Mary by the Eternal Father by singularly favouring her to be the Mother of the Incarnate Word, Jesus Christ, the Lion of Judah. Mary did not just give birth to the Son of God; she also gave birth to children of God and the generation of God-carriers. These bestowals on Mary apply to all women in particular. Pregnancy gives women the grace and opportunity to carry God and nations in their wombs. Speaking to Rebekah the wife of Isaac "the Lord said to her: 'Two nations are in your womb . . .'" – Genesis 25:23. It also applies to all the children of God in general, we are God-carriers. The book reflects on Mary as being the revelation of what God has intended all who become born again by the power of the Holy Spirit to be, God-carriers as we will see in subsequent chapters. Jesus Christ revealed this when He asked: "Who is my mother, and who are my brothers?" Pointing to his disciples, he said, "Here are my mother and my brothers. **For whoever does the will of my Father in heaven is my brother and sister and mother.**" – Mathew 12:48-50 (emphasis is mine).

Mary is revealed as the dignity of womanhood in a particular way. It is easier to reflect on the fall of man and the role of a woman in the person of Eve as in the book of

Genesis chapter three. However, the role of a woman in restoring human divinity, dignity, and naturally supernatural nature of humans and in the economy of our salvation in the person of Mary which epitomises who women truly are per the divine design, God-carriers, seems to have less emphasis among many children of God. Mary becomes the New and Last Eve since Jesus Christ is the Second and Last Adam (see 1 Corinthians 15:45-58).

The reflection in this book bears strongly on the fact that each species gives birth to its kind. Jesus Christ, as the Lion of Judah, can only be borne by a Lioness of Judah in the person of Mary. This reflection is based on the scriptural revelations and the teachings of the Church.

"The Holy Spirit illuminates the Scriptures, bringing understanding to the Word of God and revealing mysteries hidden in Scriptures. Without the Author of the Bible to shed light on the Word, we are reduced to guesswork."[1] This Author of the Bible is the Spouse of the Virgin Mary who overshadowed her and the Father of Jesus Christ. With His illumination, you can understand "the great things the Almighty has done for" (Luke 1:49) the mother of the Incarnate Word and for you consequentially as a child of God and child of Mary.

Jesus Christ revealed that believers are the light of the world. Jesus Christ was filled with the Holy Spirit and He went about doing good . . . The Holy Spirit is the Lightbulb and the Source of Light within the believers, setting them alight to become luminaries that set the world alight. It is the same Holy Spirit that switches on the believers so that they may begin to shine, "setting the world ablaze" (Acts 17:6). This same Holy Spirit is the Spouse of Mary that begot Jesus Christ,

---

[1] Bonnke, Reinhard, *Holy Spirit, Are we Flammable or Fireproof?* 2017, (eBook) p77

the Word incarnate. We should neither ignore nor disrespect such a woman.

In this book, the author deliberately uses repetitions in some places for emphasis and as an aid for the assimilation of such content.

Prologue

In the Litany of the Blessed Virgin Mary, which is also known as the Litany of Loreto, we have so many titles by which Mary is addressed. This litany was originally approved in 1587 by Pope Sixtus V. Its usage was recorded as early as 1558 at the Shrine of Our Lady of Loreto (in Italy). These titles of our Blessed Mother are not exhaustive. In 1 Corinthians 9:22b, by the Holy Spirit Paul said: "I have become all things to all people so that by all possible means I might save some." Hence, the Virgin Mary as the mother of God the Most High by grace becomes all things to all people. Scripture revealed that as Jesus Christ is so are we in this world – 1 John 4:17.

The title of Mary, the Lioness of Judah, as reflected upon in this book is as a result of the private meditations of the author. It is a title that, like other titles of Mary, stems from the fact that Mary is the mother of Jesus Christ. Reflecting on the Word of God who is God and through whom all things were created. Nothing was made that was not created by Him, through Him and for Him (John 1:1-5), I cannot help but think of the holy of holies of the temple of King Solomon.

The curtain to this holy of holies had been torn from top to bottom showing that it was not the hand of man that tore it but the hand of God. We now have open access to the holy of holies. It is no longer for the high priest to go in for us once every year. "Since we have a great high priest who has ascended into heaven, Jesus the Son of God, let us hold firmly to the faith we profess. For we do not have a high priest who is unable to empathize with our weaknesses, but we have one who has been tempted in every way, just as we are—yet he did not sin." – Hebrews 4:14-15. This High Priest has opened for us a new way into the Holy of Holies through His own body wounded and torn open for us. This body is the same body He took during His incarnation in the womb of the Blessed and Highly Favoured Virgin Mary. Brethren, "Let us then approach God's throne of grace with confidence, so that we may receive mercy and find grace to help us in our time of need." – Hebrews 4:16.

In the womb of Mary dwelt Him to whom sacrifices were offered in the holy of holies, but they did not know it; now you know it. You are highly blessed to know the Lioness of Judah. "Then turning to the disciples, Jesus said to them privately, "Blessed are the eyes that see what you see! For I tell you that many prophets and kings desired to see what you see, but did not see it, and to hear what you hear, but did not hear it." – Luke 10:23-24. As a child of God who hears the word of God and obeys it, as Mary did, you have also become a God-carrier but in a spiritual manner. Like in the case of Mary, it does not look like it, the world did not know it, yet it was true. Are you aware of this truth? We are to honour and respect this Lioness of Judah who was the first to carry the Lion of Judah both spiritually and physically. Behold the Lion of Judah, Son of the Lioness of Judah!

Jesus Christ Is the Lion of Judah

Jesus Christ after His resurrection was walking with two of his disciples on the road to Emmaus. After listening to their disappointing tale of His death and rumours about His resurrection without the disciples knowing that it was Jesus. Scripture recorded that Jesus while answering them explained to them thus: "And beginning with Moses and all the Prophets, he explained to them what was said in all the Scriptures concerning himself." – Luke 24:27.

One of those prophecies about Jesus Christ was from our patriarch, Jacob, while he was blessing his children before his death. When Jacob was speaking to Judah he said: "Judah, your brothers will praise you; your hand will be on the neck of your enemies *(see also Genesis 3:15)*; your father's sons will bow down to you. You are a lion's cub, Judah; you return from the prey, my son. Like a lion he crouches and lies down, like a lioness—who dares to rouse him? The sceptre will not depart from Judah, nor the ruler's staff from between his feet, **until he to whom it belongs shall come and the obedience of the nations shall be his**." Genesis 49:8-10 (emphasis is mine).

The prophesy states: "The sceptre will not depart from Judah, nor the ruler's staff from between his feet, until he to whom it belongs shall come and the obedience of the nations shall be his." The One "to whom it belongs" and who is to command "the obedience of the nations" is Jesus Christ (see

Luke 1:33; Psalm 72:8-11). Hence, Jesus Christ is the Lion of Judah.

This truth was later revealed in the book of Revelation: "Then one of the elders said to me, "Do not weep! **See, the Lion of the tribe of Judah, the Root of David, has triumphed.** He is able to open the scroll and its seven seals." – Revelation 5:5 (emphasis is mine).

If Jesus Christ is the Lion of Judah, which He is, what does that make His Mother, the Blessed Virgin Mary? What can give birth to a lion? Only a lioness can give birth to a lion. It then goes without saying and with no contradiction that the Blessed Virgin Mary, the Mother of Jesus Christ of Nazareth, who is the Lion of Judah is the mother of the Lion. Hence, the Virgin Mary is the Lioness of Judah.

Blessed Virgin Mary, the Mother of Jesus Christ of Nazareth, who is the Lion of Judah is the mother of the Lion. Hence, the Virgin Mary is the Lioness of Judah.

The Lioness of Judah

Mary is the Lioness of Judah; she gave birth to the Lion of Judah (Revelation 5:5). A lioness gives birth to a lion. Since Jesus Christ, according to the scriptures, is the Lion of Judah, His mother, the Blessed Virgin Mary, consequentially, is the Lioness of Judah.

It is important to note that there are things spoken about Mary, the Lioness of Judah, in the Law, the Prophets and the Psalms that we can perceive if the Spirit opens our understanding to understand the scriptures concerning the person of Mary. It is the case that there are revelations about Jesus in all the books of the Old Testament. Jesus said to His disciples: "These are the words which I spoke to you while I was still with you, that all things must be fulfilled which were written in the Law of Moses and the Prophets and the Psalms concerning Me." And He opened their understanding, that they might comprehend the Scriptures." – Luke 24:44-45. Oh, Holy Spirit, I ask that you open our understanding so that we may understand the scriptures concerning your Spouse, the Lioness of Judah. Since things are written in the Law of Moses, the Prophets and the Psalms concerning Jesus, be sure it is also the case concerning His Mother.

In the book of Genesis, immediately after the fall, a prophecy was given about Mary and her Son, Jesus Christ thus: "And I will put enmity between you and the woman, and between your offspring and hers; he will crush your head, and you will strike his heel." It is written of Mary in Psalm forty-five, verse nine: "At Your right hand stands the queen in gold from Ophir." Jesus Christ is the King of kings (Revelation 17:14) and His mother is the Queen necessarily under the law of biogenesis. The Song of Songs concerning Mary asked: "Who is she who looks forth as the morning, Fair as the moon, Clear as the sun, Awesome as an army with banners?" – Song of Songs 6:10. When Mary visited Elizabeth, Elizabeth exclaimed: "But why is this granted to me, that the mother of my Lord should come to me?" – Luke 1:43. Concerning the name of God as *Lord* that Elizabeth referred, it is written: "God also said to Moses, "I am the Lord. I appeared to Abraham, to Isaac and Jacob as God Almighty, but by my name the Lord, I did not make myself fully known to them." – Exodus 6:2-3

When Mary and Joseph presented Jesus to the temple, a prophecy was given by Simeon thus: "Then Simeon blessed them, and said to Mary His mother, "Behold, this Child is destined for the fall and rising of many in Israel, and for a sign which will be spoken against (yes, a sword will pierce through your own soul also), that the thoughts of many hearts may be revealed." – Luke 2:34-35. In the book of Judith fifteen, verse nine it is written of Mary: "You are the glory of Jerusalem, you are the great boast of Israel, you are the great pride of our nation!" Mary, on the other hand, full of the Holy Spirit said: "For He has regarded the lowly state of His maidservant; For behold, henceforth all generations will call me blessed." – Luke 1:48.

The bond between Mary and Jesus and her maternal intercession and intervention was revealed while they were at a wedding in Cana. The scripture recorded it thus: "On the third day there was a wedding in Cana of Galilee, and the mother of Jesus was there. Jesus and his disciples had also been invited to the wedding. When the wine gave out, the mother of Jesus said to him, 'They have no wine.' And Jesus said to her, 'Woman, what concern is that to you and to me? ***My hour has not yet come.*** ' His mother said to the servants, 'Do whatever he tells you.'" – John 2:5 (emphasis is mine). The result was that there was the sweetest and most abundant wine that mesmerized the attendees (see John 2:7-11).

You do not have to implicitly or explicitly ask for Mary's intercession or intervention as was the case at Cana in Galilee. However, you need to respect her and give her due honour by your words and attitude towards her as the mother of your Lord and Saviour, the Lion of Judah. Respect her as Elizabeth, the wife of Zachariah did and as John the apostle who took her to his home. Again, remember that the Spirit gave us this revelation through Mary: "Surely, from now on all generations will call me blessed; for the Mighty One has done great things for me, and holy is his name." – Luke 1:48b-49. In the order of grace, Mary is the Lioness of Judah.

The Virgin Mary Is the Lioness of Judah

The Lion of Judah was born by the Lioness of Judah. The Lion loudly roars! Never undermine the roaring of the Lioness no matter how discreet it sounds. She is a hunter! She is the mother of the Lion of Judah! She deserves to be honoured! She mirrors the dignity of womanhood in particular and humans in general. The Gospel is about Jesus Christ. Virgin Mary is like a secret garden as it is written: "My sweetheart, my bride, is a secret garden, a walled garden, a private spring." – Song of Songs 4:12 (GNT). The gospel writers don't need to write much about Mary because the role and glory of the Mother have been revealed in the Son.

Isaiah prophesying of the birth of Jesus wrote: "For to us a child is born, to us a son is given, and the government will be on his shoulders. And he will be called Wonderful Counsellor, Mighty God, Everlasting Father, Prince of Peace. Of the greatness of his government and peace, there will be no end. He will reign on David's throne and over his kingdom, establishing and upholding it with justice and righteousness from that time on and forever. The zeal of the Lord Almighty will accomplish this." Isaiah 9:6-7.

Elizabeth, speaking under the influence of the Holy Spirit as revealed in the text under consideration spoke regarding Mary thus: "When Elizabeth heard Mary's greeting, the baby leapt in her womb, and Elizabeth was filled with the Holy Spirit. In a loud voice, she exclaimed: "Blessed are you among women, and blessed is the child you will bear! But why am I so favoured, that the mother of my Lord should come to me? As soon as the sound of your greeting reached my ears, the baby in my womb leapt for joy. Blessed is she who has believed that the Lord would fulfil his promises to her!"

Mary had conceived Jesus Christ by the overshadowing power of the Holy Spirit. Hence, Mary is the Spouse of the Holy Spirit by implication. Arriving at Elizabeth's house, having been informed of God's favour towards her as regards her conception, Mary's voice alone caused mystical phenomena to take place: the child in Elizabeth's womb leapt for joy, Elizabeth was filled with the Holy Spirit, and the Holy Spirit gave her the revelation of Mary's pregnancy. The revelations given to Elizabeth concerning Mary are:

- ✓ Blessed is Mary among women.
- ✓ Blessed is the child that Mary will bear (Jesus Christ).
- ✓ Elizabeth was privileged to be visited by Mary.
- ✓ John rejoiced in her womb.
- ✓ Mary is the mother of her Lord (the mother of God).
- ✓ Mary is blessed by believing and obeying the word of God; that the Lord will fulfil his promises to her.

The above enumerated were revealed to Elizabeth by the Holy Spirit just as the Angel revealed to Mary that Elizabeth was pregnant. Mary, also full of the Holy Spirit responded: "My soul glorifies the Lord, and my spirit rejoices in God my Savior, for he has been mindful of the humble state of his servant. From now on all generations will call me blessed, for the Mighty One has done great things for me—holy is his name." – Luke 1:46-49.

Jesus Christ as the Lion of Judah commands the obedience of the nations. As His rule shall have no end, in the same vein, all generations shall call His Mother Blessed. She is the Lioness of Judah by implication.

Again, Jesus Christ came to fulfil all the laws and the prophets. Mary is also his mother by the law and the prophets. Apart from other laws, Mary, the mother of Jesus Christ, is the Lioness of Judah in line with the biogenesis law.

Virgin Mary is like a secret garden as it is written: "My sweetheart, my bride, is a secret garden, a walled garden, a private spring." – Song of Songs 4:12

The Biogenesis Law and the Lioness of Judah

The law of biogenesis states that it is from life that life emanates. This is in line with the proposition of observational science according to which every organism reproduces fellow organisms following their kind. Agreeingly, Genesis chapter one revealed how God created the varied kinds of life on earth and made them reproduce after their kind.[2] Hence, in this first chapter of the book of Genesis, when God created everything that exists it was recorded thus: "And God said, "Let the water teem with living creatures, and let birds fly above the earth across the vault of the sky." So, God created the great creatures of the sea and every living thing with which the water teems and that moves about in it, according to their kinds, and every winged bird according to its kind. And God saw that it was good. God blessed them and said, "Be fruitful and increase in number and fill the water in the seas, and let the birds increase on the earth." And there was evening, and there was morning—the fifth day.

And God said, "Let the land produce living creatures according to their kinds: the livestock, the creatures that move along the ground, and the wild animals, each according to its kind." And it was so. God made the wild animals according to their kinds, the livestock according to their kinds, and all the

---

[2] Lisle, Jason, "God & Natural Law", https://answersingenesis.org/is-god-real/god-natural-law/, accessed on 14/06/2024.

creatures that move along the ground according to their kinds. And God saw that it was good." – Genesis 1:20-25

According to this record, we understand that all the sea creatures, all the air creatures and all the land creatures were created to reproduce according to their kinds. Hence, a monkey gives birth to a monkey, a snake gives birth to a snake, a whale gives birth to a whale, a starfish gives birth to a starfish, a goat gives birth to a goat, a dog gives birth to a dog and so on.

Regarding human beings, when God wanted to create human beings, it was recorded: Then God said, "Let us make mankind in our image, in our likeness, so that they may rule over the fish in the sea and the birds in the sky, over the livestock and all the wild animals, and over all the creatures that move along the ground." So, God created mankind in his own image, in the image of God he created them; male and female he created them. God blessed them and said to them, "Be fruitful and increase in number; fill the earth and subdue it. Rule over the fish in the sea and the birds in the sky and over every living creature that moves on the ground." – Genesis 1: 26-28

It means that human beings give birth to human beings. In order words, the image and likeness of God give birth to the image and likeness of God. Concerning human beings the Psalmist said: "I praise you because I am fearfully and wonderfully made; your works are wonderful; I know that full well." – Psalm 139:14. This is also to say that when human beings give birth, they give birth to that which is fearfully and wonderfully made; they give birth to that which "is very good" (Genesis 1:31).

Once again, regarding human beings, the Psalmist gave us this revelation: "I have said, Ye are gods; and all of you are children of the most High." – Psalm 82:6. It should not be surprising that we are gods and the children of the most High because God made us in his image and likeness. It is also not surprising that Mary is the Mother of God because she is in the image and likeness of God as we all are. Holy Spirit through the apostle John further revealed concerning us thus: "Beloved, now we are children of God; and it has not yet been revealed what we shall be, but we know that when He is revealed, we shall be like Him, for we shall see Him as He is." When anyone calls God their Father, they should be aware of the implications of what they are saying in line with every kind begets their kind. Hence, "Man, know yourself!" You are a child of God. You are a child of Mary, and your brother is Jesus Christ of Nazareth, the First-Born Son (see Romans 8:29b).

In line with the law of biogenesis, the Lion of Judah can only be born by the Lioness of Judah. Mary is the Lioness of Judah. The scripture revealed to us that Jesus Christ is the prophesied Lion of Judah as shown above. Again, Mary's character reveals that she is the Lioness of Judah.

The Lioness Character in Cana

Mary displayed her lioness character in Cana when she was at a wedding feast with Jesus Christ and His disciples. Before discussing what happened at that wedding feast, let us take a look at the character of a lioness.

Imara Njeri, in one of her articles, called a lioness "An Unsung Hero of the Pride". How well that title implicitly describes the Virgin Mary! Mary can be called an Unsung Hero of our Salvation. Writing about a lioness, Imara Njeri wrote: "She is a figure of strength, but her strength is rooted in her gentleness. While she is an expert hunter able to outsmart her prey and take down a target twice her size, she is also a devoted mother, protecting her cubs and teaching them the skills they need to survive. The lioness displays a powerful balance between ferocity and compassion. She invests her energy in meticulous grooming that forges unbreakable bonds, and her strength is manifested in the unity she fosters and the leadership she provides."[3]

With this image of a lioness in our mind, I would like us to have a look at what Mary did at the wedding at Cana in Galilee: "On the third day, a wedding took place at Cana in Galilee. Jesus' mother was there, and Jesus and his disciples had also been invited to the wedding. When the wine was gone, Jesus' mother said to him, "They have no more wine."

---

[3] https://ishara.ke/the-lioness-an-unsung-hero-of-the-pride/#:~:text=She%20is%20a%20figure%20of,skills%20they%20need%20to%20survive. (assessed 28/05/2024)

"Woman, why do you involve me?" Jesus replied. "My hour has not yet come." His mother said to the servants, "Do whatever he tells you." Nearby stood six stone water jars, the kind used by the Jews for ceremonial washing, each holding from twenty to thirty gallons. Jesus said to the servants, "Fill the jars with water"; so, they filled them to the brim. Then he told them, "Now draw some out and take it to the master of the banquet." "They did so, and the master of the banquet tasted the water that had been turned into wine. He did not realize where it had come from, though the servants who had drawn the water knew. Then he called the bridegroom aside and said, "Everyone brings out the choice wine first and then the cheaper wine after the guests have had too much to drink; but you have saved the best till now." – John 2:1-10

Mary had been invited together with Jesus and His disciples to this wedding feast. They ran out of wine. Mary was concerned and did not want the bride and groom to be embarrassed. She, knowing what her Son could do, approached him so that He may help. Jesus made it clear to Mary that His time for performing miracles had not yet come.

A lioness in the jungle takes care of her cubs. Like the Lioness that she is, Mary refused to let her children be embarrassed on their wedding day. She gently and smartly turned to the servants and instructed them to do whatever Jesus told them. The Lioness is a hunter! Concerning asking, the word of God says: "Therefore I say to you, whatever things you ask when you pray, believe that you receive them, and you will have them." – Mark 11:24. Mary had asked, and nothing can stop her from getting what she had asked for, not even the God's timing.

What was the result of this intervention and intercession from Mary? Firstly, Jesus performed His first miracle that provoked faith from his disciples who were still new. "What

Jesus did here in Cana of Galilee was the first of the signs through which he revealed his glory; and his disciples believed in him." – John 2:11. Mary's intercession and intervention launched Jesus' mission, as it were, and revealed him to his disciples and non-disciples as well.

How often have I heard ministers of the gospel tell of this event and either ignore completely the role of Mary or make very light of it? This Lioness of Judah shifted God's timing, not for her benefit but for the benefit of her children who invited her to their wedding feast. It is also worth noting that the wedding couple did not ask for Mary's intervention. By merely inviting her, she saw their need and intervened even without their knowledge and asking. She is still doing the same today.

This is one of the reasons her children consecrate themselves to her and seek her intervention and intercession because even now she can still intercede and shift God's timing for her children's miracle. She was with Jesus at Cana's wedding when she did this. She can do much more now that she is with Him in heaven. Mary is the Lioness of Judah! Her character as the Lioness was also revealed at Calvary.

> "She is a figure of strength, but her strength is rooted in her gentleness. While she is an expert hunter . . . she is also a devoted mother, protecting her cubs and teaching them the skills they need to survive. The lioness displays a powerful balance between ferocity and compassion." - Imara Njeri

The Lioness Character at Calvary

Mary together with Joseph, presenting the infant Jesus to the temple encountered Simeon and prophetess Anna. Among the prophesies they were given Simeon turned to Mary and said: "This child is destined to cause the falling and rising of many in Israel, and to be a sign that will be spoken against, so that the thoughts of many hearts will be revealed. And a sword will pierce your own soul too." – Luke 2: 34-35

If not that as a Lioness, "she is a figure of strength" it would have been easier to back off at this stage hearing that "a sword will pierce your own soul too." Instead, Mary remained determined more than ever to raise this Child in the fear of God and to grow in favour before God and man (see Luke 2:52).

On the day Jesus was crucified, it was written: "Near the cross of Jesus stood his mother, his mother's sister, Mary the wife of Clopas, and Mary Magdalene. When Jesus saw his mother there, and the disciple whom he loved standing nearby, he said to her, "Woman, here is your son," and to the disciple, "Here is your mother." From that time on, this disciple took her into his home." – John 19:25-27

Prophet Isaiah describing the passion, and the torture that Jesus received wrote: "His appearance was so disfigured beyond that of any human being and his form marred beyond human likeness." Isaiah 52:14b. What mother will stand to witness her son thus tortured and killed in the most ignominious way and was still standing? It is only that mother who is a Lioness. Mary is the Lioness of Judah! When the prophecy was spoken from the lips of Simeon that a sword would pierce her soul too, she received the grace to be a co-victim with her Son, the Lion of Judah. This Lion respected His Lioness.

Jesus' Respect for His Mother

Some people who tend to disrespect or disregard this Unsung Hero of our Salvation, this Lioness of Judah sometimes cite an incident that happened in the gospel. It is written thus: "While Jesus was still talking to the crowd, his mother and brothers stood outside, wanting to speak to him. Someone told him, "Your mother and brothers are standing outside, wanting to speak to you." He replied to him, "Who is my mother, and who are my brothers?" Pointing to his disciples, he said, "Here are my mother and my brothers. For whoever does the will of my Father in heaven is my brother and sister and mother." – Matthew 12:46-50

Of course, Jesus meant what He said when He said that "whoever does the will of His Father in heaven is His brother and sister and mother". Here, Jesus reveals that Mary is not just her mother merely by their biological link but as a result of her obedience to the Word and her total surrender to the will of the Father. Here, Jesus is repeating what the Holy Spirit revealed to Elizabeth regarding Mary when she said: "Blessed is she who has believed that the Lord would fulfil his promises to her!"

Bearing in mind that Jesus Christ is the one who gave us the commandment to obey our father and mother, it will be inconceivable that He will disobey the commandment He gave through Moses. "Honour your father and your mother, so that you may live long in the land the Lord your God is giving you." Exodus 20:12

The scripture also made us understand that Jesus Christ was obedient to His parents: "Then he went down to Nazareth with them and was obedient to them (i.e. Mary and Joseph). But his mother treasured all these things in her heart. And Jesus grew in wisdom and stature, and in favour with God and man." – Luke 1:51-52

Jesus revealed that as Mary carried him in her womb for nine months, we can equally carry him within us for our entire life here on earth by doing what Mary did: "by doing the will of our Father in heaven". We know that the will of our Father being spoken of is the word of God. God's will and his word cannot be different. God expresses his will through his word. When that word came to Mary, she received it, believed it and did it which was demonstrated when she hurriedly went to visit Elizabeth to take care of her and her unborn child. That is doing the word of God; that is doing the will of the Father – "love as I have loved you" – John 13:34-35. We are to imitate Jesus Christ, the Lion of Judah among other things in His respect towards the Lioness of Judah.

Be Imitators of the Lion of Judah

The scripture urged us to be imitators of God (Ephesians 5:1). Jesus Christ honoured, respected and obeyed His mother. As His brothers and sisters, we should love, honour and respect the mother of our Lord and Saviour. Natural and supernatural instinct urges us to give respect to the one that respect is due. The wordings of the angel sent by the Eternal Father to the Lioness of Judah epitomises respect and honour: "In the sixth month, the angel Gabriel was sent by God to a town in Galilee called Nazareth, to a virgin engaged to a man whose name was Joseph, of the house of David. The virgin's name was Mary. And he came to her and said, 'Greetings, favoured one! The Lord is with you." – Luke 1:26-28. What an honour and respect!

When we talk about the past and present prophets, we speak about them with great respect. We have seen God honouring men and women who walked or are walking with Him. "Enoch walked faithfully with God; then he was no more because God took him away." – Genesis 5:24. Again it is written: "Abraham believed God, and it was credited to him as righteousness, and he was called God's friend." – James 2:23. Did Virgin Mary walk with God? Did the Virgin Mary believe God? Sure, she did! She is the Lioness of Judah, the mother of the Lion of Judah. She is highly favoured and honoured by God. You should honour her too as a child of God and her child.

I need to point out that you do not need to ask Mary to intercede or intervene for you. However, but you need to speak of her with the utmost honour, respect and admiration. Why? She is the mother of your Lord, Jesus Christ. Consider the queens of this world, the mothers and wives of political leaders, the mothers and wives of the men of God you honour.

Mothers and Wives of Men and Women of God We Honour

Within the Christian circle, no one will speak lightly or disrespectfully of the wife or mother of their general overseer, pastor or priest. No one equally can speak lightly or disrespectfully of the wife or mother of the general overseers' spiritual father or mother and any person they hold in honour. Respect is given to the mothers and wives of the political leaders. Why then can any Christian speak lightly or disrespectfully about Mary, the mother of Jesus Christ?

In the world, when a man is elected as a president in most countries, their wife becomes automatically the most respected woman in the country. She will start going by the name of a First Lady. The same can be said of women whose husbands were elected as governors of states. Consequentially, the mothers of the elected political leaders become women of great honour. In some countries, it is a crime to speak disrespectfully against the members of a royal family. Why should someone who has been saved by Jesus Christ, who takes Jesus Christ as their personal Lord and Saviour speak lightly or disrespectfully of His mother? It does not matter your Christian denomination or affiliation, there is no excuse to dishonour the mother of the Lion of Judah. How can you disrespect the Mother in whose womb lay the Lion for nine months? Yet, we honour, respect, admire and visit the land trodden upon by the Lion of Judah and where Mary gave birth to Him.

Once again, how is it that you admire, respect and hold in high regard the wives and mothers of your general overseers and yet disrespect Mary? How do you honour, visit or yearn to visit the land where Jesus was born and disrespect her that gave birth to him in that land?

Lioness of Judah and the Holy Land of Israel

The land of Israel is holy because God chose it and dwelt therein. Jerusalem is holy and revered because God chose it and inhabited it and continues to inhabit it. The scripture says: "The Lord has chosen Jerusalem; he wants it for his home. He says, "This is my resting place forever. Here is where I want to stay." – Psalm 132:13-14. How then do you visit and love and honour the land chosen by God where Jesus lived and walked and ignore the woman in whose womb he stayed for nine months and who he lived with for 30 years out of 33 years he lived on earth? Jesus lived under her authority and obeyed her. Mary is the one who gave birth to Him in this land.

Moreover, the Lord chose Mary of all women on earth for the incarnation of His Son. She should be honoured and respected. On the other hand, the Lord has also chosen to dwell in you: "Jesus answered him, 'Those who love me will keep my word, and my Father will love them, and we will come to them and make our home with them." – John 14:23. And again He said: "Listen! I am standing at the door, knocking; if you hear my voice and open the door, I will come into you and eat with you, and you with me." – Revelation 3:20. As He inhabited Mary and the land of Israel, He wants also to dwell in you and sop with you.

Respect and honour her in whom the Word first dwelt as He dwells in you now. Your body is God's temple! (1 Corinthians 6:19-20). The womb of the Blessed Virgin Mary, the Lioness of Judah was a resting place for the Lion of Judah for at least nine months before He came out to roar. She deserves reverence and honour; don't you think so?

The Lioness who breastfed the Lion of Judah and suckled Him for His sustenance on earth deserves honour and respect. Mary is the Lady that the Lion of Judah lived with more than anyone else on earth. She is the one who cooked for him and fed him. She nurtured him to grow in favour before God and man. The Lioness of Judah deserves every honour and respect humans can render apart from to God, don't you think so? She is the Lioness of Judah! As a lioness hunts and protects her cubs, Mary intercedes and intervenes for her children.

Mary's Intercession and Intervention

You do not have to ask your pastor, priest or prophet to pray for or with you. This is to say that you do not have to ask the saints triumphant, the saints suffering or other saints militants to pray for you. Hence, you do not have to ask for Mary's intercession and intervention. Asking for Mary's intercession or intervention is never a requirement for you to be a true child of God. No! She is not requiring you to ask for her intercession or intervention. It is entirely up to you to ask for her maternal intervention if you feel that you need her help. You can call upon and invite her into your life and situations. Otherwise, you can ask directly from the Father in the Name of our Lord and Saviour Jesus Christ. The Father himself loves you and you do not have to ask through anyone – John 16:27.

In the same vein, the Eternal Father is almighty. He does not have to use or pass through Mary for the incarnation of the Word for our redemption. God came directly to Moses on the Mount. He spoke with Moses face to face as a man speaks with a friend (see Exodus 33:11). Yet, God chose to honour, and highly favour Mary by needing her both to give birth and to nurture His Son, Jesus Christ. You are free to choose too.

You see, at the wedding at Cana in Galilee, the couple never asked for her intervention or intercession. They invited her as a relation of theirs and she came with Jesus and Jesus came with his disciples. Without being asked, she noticed that their wine had run out. She didn't want them to be embarrassed. Knowing what Jesus can do, she went to Jesus and asked for his intervention. You are a member of the household of God as scripture revealed: "So then you are no longer strangers and aliens, but you are citizens with the saints and also members of the household of God" – Ephesians 2:19 – we have Mary, the mother of Jesus Christ as our Mother in this household. You can invite her if you choose to into whatever you are doing as the couple invited her to their wedding at Cana in Galilee.

When Mary intervened at the wedding, the answer Jesus gave her seemed not encouraging. However, she, being a Lioness, cannot be deterred. She turned to the servants and asked them to do what she had been doing all her life that caused the Word to become incarnate in her: "Whatever He asks you to do, do it!" Her intercession and her intervention caused God's timing to be changed. She can do the same for you when you honour, respect and invite her even without asking for her intervention and intercession. Should the one who can change God's timing, who caused Jesus to produce His first sign, the Lioness of Judah, not deserve your respect and honour? I think she should be honoured!

Mary's intercession is never about her honour and glorification. At the wedding, they did not turn around to start thanking her and admire how powerful and wonderful she was. Apart from the servants she spoke to, many did not even know the role she played. She was as discreet as a secret garden. Behold the result of her intervention at this wedding: "What Jesus did here in Cana of Galilee was the first of the signs through which he revealed his glory; and his disciples believed in him." – John 2:11. The Lioness of Judah's intercession is about revealing of Jesus' glory and about causing his disciples to believe, not in her, but in Jesus Christ. If you truly love and respect Jesus, do not speak ill of this

Woman, do not disrespect her! You do not have to ask her to intercede for you and you also do not have to have anything to do with her statue or images. Simply respect her. Do not slight her by your words or attitudes.

Statues and Images of Mary the Lioness of Judah

It is never a requirement to have a statue or any image of Mary, the Lioness of Judah for it to be that you love and respect her. Having her statue and images are not necessarily a guarantee that you love her. Some people honour their man and woman of God by having their pictures all over their possessions, framed or in stickers. We also have those who though they love their man or woman of God do not have their pictures in any of their possessions. Not having such pictures does not necessarily mean that they love them less. It is simply their choice.

No woman or man of God can ever be compared to the Blessed Virgin Mary's intimacy and favour with God, the mother of Jesus Christ. Having her images is not necessarily denominationally dependent. No! If you wish to express your love for her by having her images, it is up to you. On the other hand, if you wish to express your love for her by not having her images, it is also entirely up to you. However, we should not condemn each other. Her images are never for worship just as the pictures and images of our men and women of God or any other picture we cherish are not and should not be for worship.

Bodily, the Lioness was present during the advent of the Holy Spirit and the inauguration of the Church.

Lioness of Judah in Catholicism and Pentecostalism

Mary, the Lioness of Judah, in union with the Holy Spirit, gave birth to the incarnate Word for our salvation. She was present with the disciples while they waited for the descent of the Holy Spirit for the birth of the Church. This Church is to go all over the world to witness that Jesus is alive (see Acts 1:8). John the apostle while in the spirit saw the son of man. He recorded: "When I saw him, I fell at his feet as though dead. Then he placed his right hand on me and said: 'Do not be afraid. I am the First and the Last. I am the Living One; I was dead, and now look, I am alive for ever and ever! And I hold the keys of death and Hades." – Revelation 1:17-18.

The Church taught us that "After her Son's Ascension, Mary 'aided the beginnings of the Church by her prayers.' In her association with the apostles and several women, 'we also see Mary by her prayers imploring the gift of the Spirit, who had already overshadowed her in the Annunciation.'" – (CCC), para 965.

This Lioness, who in union with the Holy Spirit gave us the incarnate Word, our Saviour, was active with the body of Christ while they eagerly waited for the descent of the Holy Spirit to be empowered for the great commission (see Mark 16:15-16). This same Lioness is still active while the body of Christ is carrying out this great commission, doing the same thing she had been doing, in wedding at Cana and at the Upper Room.

Honouring Mary should not be a mark of being a Catholic. Anyone of any denomination can honour Mary. Of course, many other Christian denominations honour and respect her. No matter how you choose to honour her, it is up to you as long as you are not violating the dictates of the Scriptures and the Magisterium of the Church. Mary is present in the entire history of the economy of our salvation. Mary was not just present but was part and parcel and at the heart of every step of our salvation. How can you sideline or slight such a woman?

God can do without Mary, but He did not. You can do without Mary, but you should not. Why? Because God did not do without her. If God considers her important in the plan for the salvation of the human race, we should take her very seriously. Though we know Jesus Christ no longer in the flesh, the fact that he came in the flesh necessitates our honouring her through whom he came in the flesh. Despising and slighting Mary is inadvertently despising and slighting the incarnation of her Son, Jesus Christ. Yet, without the incarnation, the price of our redemption would not have been paid. Mary played a pivotal role in every stage of our salvation. Without the incarnation, there would not have been passion and the resurrection. Think about that and respect her. Lioness gave birth to the Lion of Judah and nurtured Him and He lived with her for at least 30 years.

The Lioness Gave Birth to the Lion of Judah

Eternal Father consulted with Mary, with only Mary, when the Word was to take flesh for our salvation. It was for the salvation of all human beings not just Christians, not just Catholics: "And He Himself is the propitiation for our sins, and not for ours only but also for the whole world." – 1 John 2:2. As such, all human beings are supposed to be honouring this woman whom God honoured by consulting her regarding the incarnation of the Word for our salvation. It was recorded in the scripture thus:

"Now in the sixth month, the angel Gabriel was sent by God to a city of Galilee named Nazareth, to a virgin betrothed to a man whose name was Joseph, of the house of David. The virgin's name was Mary. And having come in, the angel said to her, "Rejoice, highly favoured one, the Lord is with you; blessed are you among women!"

But when she saw him, she was troubled at his saying, and considered what manner of greeting this was. Then the angel said to her, "Do not be afraid, Mary, for you have found favour with God. And behold, you will conceive in your womb and bring forth a Son and shall call His name Jesus. He will be great and will be called the Son of the Highest; and the Lord God will give Him the throne of His father David. And He will reign over the house of Jacob forever, and of His kingdom there will be no end."

Then Mary said to the angel, "How can this be, since I do not know a man?" And the angel answered and said to her,

"The Holy Spirit will come upon you, and the power of the Highest will overshadow you; therefore, also, that Holy One who is to be born will be called the Son of God. Now indeed, Elizabeth your relative has also conceived a son in her old age; and this is now the sixth month for her who was called barren. For with God nothing will be impossible." Then Mary said, "Behold the maidservant of the Lord! Let it be to me according to your word." And the angel departed from her." – Luke 1:26-38

You can see that the Lion of Judah was to be born. God spotted a Lioness of Judah in the person of Mary and sent His angel to announce to her that she had been chosen to give birth to the Lion of Judah.

It is quite interesting that Jesus Christ said: "Then said Jesus to them again, "Peace be unto you. As My Father hath sent Me, even so send I you." – John 20:21. How did the Father send Jesus? Through Mary. That is how it is, it cannot be otherwise. If you are a Christian, no matter your denomination, you are a Christian through this Lioness of Judah whether you know it or not, whether you acknowledge it or not. Jesus Christ, coming for our salvation, came through the Lioness of Judah.

This is another interesting revelation that should cause you to deeply reverence this Lioness of Judah: When Jesus Christ was incarnated in the womb of the Blessed Virgin Mary, you were incarnated with Him therein. When Jesus was living in the house of Mary being breastfed, nurtured, fed and instructed to grow in favour before God and men, you were inside Jesus. When He was undergoing the passion, crucified on the cross, died and laid buried in the tomb, you were inside him. When he resurrected, you resurrected with him. When he is seated at the right hand of the Father, you are seated with him.

The Holy Spirit revealed this in the book of Colossians when He said: "In Him you were also circumcised with the circumcision made without hands. . . . buried with Him in baptism, in which you also were raised with Him through faith in the working of God, who raised Him from the dead." – Colossians 2:11-12. Again in the book of Ephesians the Spirit also revealed: "But God, who is rich in mercy, because of His great love with which He loved us, even when we were dead in trespasses, made us alive together with Christ (by grace you have been saved), and raised us up together, and made us sit together in the heavenly places in Christ Jesus, that in the ages to come He might show the exceeding riches of His grace in His kindness toward us in Christ Jesus." – Ephesian 2:4-7.

We would not have died with him when he died if we had not been in him from the very moment of his incarnation. We have been in Jesus Christ from the very moment of his incarnation to this very moment. This Spirit also revealed that it is "in him we live and move and have our being.' As some of your own poets have said, 'We are his offspring." – Acts 17:28. If we are Jesus' offspring, it implies that we are the offspring of Mary; it does not matter what denomination you belong to. The Lioness of Judah was present when we were being crucified together with the Lion of Judah.

The Lioness at Sacrificial Death of the Lion

During the sacrificial death and resurrection of Jesus Christ, Mary was there. It was as if she was there, joining in offering Jesus Christ, her son, to the eternal Father for our salvation. Otherwise, why should a mother be present to watch her son killed in such an ignominious manner? "Near the cross of Jesus stood his mother, his mother's sister, Mary the wife of Clopas, and Mary Magdalene." – John 19:25.

This Lioness of Judah, so strong and courageous to stand by her son that was crucified deserve every honour and respect, don't you agree? Her presence at the Calvary also fulfilled the prophecy made when Jesus as an infant was presented to the temple: "Yes, a sword will pierce through your own soul also, that the thoughts of many hearts may be revealed." – Luke 2:35. Why this prophecy? It is for our sake, those of us who are Christians and for the entire human race for whom Jesus died. She deserves honour and respect, doesn't she?

The salvific sword of love that pierced the soul of Jesus Christ for our sake pierced her soul too in fulfilment of the prophecy. Her love for you was unshakable and unquenchable that she stood in support of her Son during His sacrificial death for us. The Lioness of Judah is the mother of Love (see 1 John 4:16). It was then not surprising that she was present on Pentecost Day.

Behold Lioness Prior and On the Pentecost Day

It was revealed in the scripture thus: "Then the apostles returned to Jerusalem from the hill called the Mount of Olives, a Sabbath day's walk from the city. When they arrived, they went upstairs to the room where they were staying. Those present were Peter, John, James and Andrew; Philip and Thomas, Bartholomew and Matthew; James son of Alphaeus and Simon the Zealot, and Judas son of James. They all joined together constantly in prayer, along with the women and Mary the mother of Jesus, and with his brothers." – Acts 1:12-14. The number of those present, praying constantly with Mary while waiting for the outpouring of the Holy Spirit were one hundred and twenty in number – Acts 1:15.

The descent of the Holy Spirit upon the disciples of Jesus Christ on the Pentecost day is regarded as the birth of the Church or the Epiphany of the Church or both. The apostles and disciples of Jesus Christ, at this most critical moment in the history of the Church, did not ignore Mary, how then can you say that you are Pentecostal, Evangelical or any other denominational name and you ignore Mary that the Pillars and Foundations of the Church did not ignore? They honoured and respected her. They were full of the Holy Spirit, speaking in other tongues and were still honouring and respecting Mary. Mary was in their midst.

She was instrumental in the incarnation of the Word. The Lioness of Judah was also present during the fulfilment of the words of the incarnate Word regarding the coming of Another

Helper just like Himself, the Holy Spirit. Remember that it is the same Holy Spirit that overshadowed her for the incarnation of the Word. While on the cross, Jesus Christ bequeathed Mary to us as our Mother through John the apostle. Behold, John took her home.

The Apostle John Took Mary Home

Holy Spirit, through the apostle Paul said: "Even if you had ten thousand guardians in Christ, you do not have many fathers, for in Christ Jesus I became your father through the gospel. Therefore, I urge you to imitate me." It was repeated again thus: "Imitate me, just as I imitate Christ." – 1 Corinthians 4:15-16; 11:1. In the same spirit I can say that even though you might have many Mums in the Lord and many First Ladies in the Lord, Mary, the Lioness of Judah, became our Blessed Mother by the virtue of her motherhood of Christ Jesus, the Lion of Judah. As apostle John took her home, I urge you, therefore, to imitate him; take Mary home too. Let us suppose that you do not want to take her home, respect and honour her duly. The Lioness of Judah is our Mother in the order of grace.

Yes, an apostle, in the person of John the Evangelist, took Mary home: "Now there stood by the cross of Jesus His mother, and His mother's sister, Mary the wife of Clopas, and Mary Magdalene. When Jesus therefore saw His mother, and the disciple whom He loved standing by, He said to His mother, "Woman, behold your son!" Then He said to the disciple, "Behold your mother!" And from that hour that disciple took her to his own home." – John 19:25-27.

St John, one of the twelve apostles of Jesus Christ, one of the pillars of our faith took Mary to his home and lived with her. Hence, Jesus Christ lived with Mary, honouring, respecting obeying and living under her authority. Apostle John took Mary to his home and lived with her. You too should take Mary home if you are following the example of the apostles, imitating them. Remember that the apostles are the cornerstone upon which we are built. The scripture says: "For it is through Him (Jesus Christ) that we both have a direct way of approach in one Spirit to the Father. So then you are no longer strangers and aliens, outsiders without rights of citizenship, but you are fellow citizens with the saints (God's people), and are members of God's household, having been built on the foundation of the apostles and prophets, with Christ Jesus Himself as the chief Cornerstone, in whom the whole structure is joined together, and it continues to increase growing into a holy temple in the Lord, a sanctuary dedicated, set apart, and sacred to the presence of the Lord. In Him and in fellowship with one another you also are being built together into a dwelling place of God in the Spirit." – Ephesians 2:18-22

We need to always bear in mind that we have direct access to the Father through Jesus Christ. We do not have to have intermediaries in the persons of the Virgin Mary, the Lioness of Judah, the saints or angels. However, in the spirit they are gatekeepers, and they can help you have access to certain graces easier and possibly quicker as was the case at the wedding at Cana in Galilee. Again, though our Eternal Father can, and most times do attend to us directly, in most cases He uses intermediaries to meet our needs. He used Mary for Jesus to incarnate for our salvation. Father used an angel to deliver the message of our salvation to Mary. Angels were also used in delivering messages to the shepherds, St Joseph and the Magi. God also used the apostles and disciples to give us His word in a written form.

However, as the apostles are our foundation with the prophets, we need to watch out for what they did and do the same. One of the things they did was that they respected and honoured Mary when Jesus handed her over to them. They took her home. Again since "In Jesus Christ and in fellowship with one another you also are being built together into a dwelling place of God in the Spirit" we need to look up to her in whom the Incarnate Word ever first dwelt.

The Lioness as the highly favoured of the Lord, she can influence divine timing.

Mary's Influence on God's Kairos (Timing)

For those Christians, Catholics and others alike, who ask for Mary's intercession and intervention, it is because of a secret that they discovered, knowing or unknowing. Mary has a special privilege or favour to influence God's timing. Immediately Mary was born, God's timing began ticking for the incarnation of His Word. When Mary reached the age of childbirth, it instantly became God's timing for the birth of Jesus Christ, our Saviour. When Mary intervened at the wedding at Cana in Galilee, it became God's timing for the first sign and miracle of Jesus Christ.

The Meaning of Kairos and Chronos
Kairos (Greek: καιρός) is an old Greek word that means "the right" or "opportune moment" or "the absolute moment". Kairos in the New Testament means "the appointed time in God's purpose", and "the God's appointed time for Him to act". For instance, when Jesus started His public ministry, it was recorded thus: "The time has come," he said. "The kingdom of God has come near. Repent and believe the good news!"

On the other hand, Chronos (Greek: Χρόνος) is the measure of quantitative time or an exact time. There are 53 instances it is used in the scriptures in this context. For instance, it was recorded: "Then Herod called the Magi secretly and found out from them the exact time the star had appeared." – Matthew 2:7. In Acts it was also recorded: "He said to them: "It is not for you to know the times or dates the Father has set by his own authority." – Acts 1:7.

Apart from the incarnation of the Word in Mary, her intervention at the wedding in Cana in Galilee revealed to us that she has tremendous irresistible power, privilege, and favour to manipulate God's Kairos (timing) to favour those who seek her intercession, intervention or who merely invited her in other to reveal God's glory and elicit faith in God among the disciples. As a Lioness, her roar may not be so loud but do not mistake it for weakness for she is a hunter for the Eternal Father. This is what she exhibited at the wedding at Cana in Galilee.

It is a great privilege to be associated with Mary, the Lioness of Judah.

Privileged to be Visited by the Lioness of Judah

Elizabeth, the wife of Zachariah felt privileged to be visited by the Lioness of Judah, the mother of the Lord. The scripture recorded Mary's visit thus: "It happened, when Elizabeth heard the greeting of Mary, that the babe leapt in her womb; and Elizabeth was filled with the Holy Spirit. Then she spoke out with a loud voice and said, "Blessed are you among women, and blessed is the fruit of your womb! **But why is this granted to me, that the mother of my Lord should come to me?** For indeed, as soon as the voice of your greeting sounded in my ears, the babe leapt in my womb for joy. Blessed is she who believed, for there will be a fulfilment of those things which were told her from the Lord." – Luke 1:41-45 (Emphasis is mine).

On receiving this incredible praise, respect and honour, Mary responded: "My soul magnifies the Lord, And my spirit has rejoiced in God my Savior. For He has regarded the lowly state of His maidservant; For behold, henceforth all generations will call me blessed.

For He who is mighty has done great things for me, And holy is His name. And His mercy is on those who fear Him From generation to generation.

He has shown strength with His arm; He has scattered the proud in the imagination of their hearts. He has put down the mighty from their thrones and exalted the lowly.

He has filled the hungry with good things, And the rich He has sent away empty. He has helped His servant Israel, In remembrance of His mercy, As He spoke to our fathers, To Abraham and to his seed forever."

In Mary's response, we see her returning all glory to God when she was acknowledged, respected and honoured. She turns the focus of the children of God to be focused on God the author and finisher of our faith (see Hebrews 12:2). Mary is the Mother in the family of God in the order of grace.

The Lioness of Judah is the Mother of Christians

Mary is the mother of our Lord, Jesus Christ who is the Lion of Judah. Christians are the brethren, brothers and sisters of Jesus Christ. It can be said that Christians are children of Mary.

The mystery of Mary's motherhood of the Mystical Body of Christ was luminously revealed through the teaching of the Church thus:

"Mary's role in the Church is inseparable from her union with Christ and flows directly from it. 'This union of the other with the Son in the work of salvation is made manifest from the time of Christ's virginal conception up to his death', it is made manifest above all at the hour of his Passion:

Thus, the Blessed Virgin advanced in her pilgrimage of faith, and faithfully persevered in her union with her Son unto the cross. There she stood, in keeping with the divine plan, enduring with her only begotten Son the intensity of his suffering, joining herself with his sacrifice in her mother's heart, and lovingly consenting to the immolation of this victim born of her: to be given, by the same Christ Jesus dying on the cross, as a mother to his disciple, with these words: 'Woman, behold your son.'"[4]

However, some may argue against being children of Mary thus: "From now on, we regard no one according to the flesh. Even though we have known Christ according to the

---

[4] Chapman, Geoffrey, *Catechism of the Catholic Church [CCC]*, 1994, para 964

flesh, yet now we know Him thus no longer. Therefore, if anyone is in Christ, he is a new creation; old things have passed away; behold, all things have become new." – 2 Corinthians 5:16-17. This applies relevantly to our originating from Adam and Eve and their fall from grace. Hence, someone may be tempted to postulate that though Mary gave birth to Jesus in the flesh, we no longer know Jesus according to the flesh. As such, we are not to regard his mother according to the flesh as our mother nor associate with her. This position can only seem tenable if one forgets the nature of Christ's birth. Though Jesus was born in the flesh and was fully human, it was not necessarily according to the manner of the flesh but by the power of the Holy Spirit.

Concerning the conception of Jesus Christ the Spirit gave us this revelation: "And the angel answered and said to her, "The Holy Spirit will come upon you, and the power of the Highest will overshadow you; therefore, also, that Holy One who is to be born will be called the Son of God." – Luke 1:35. This revealed that Jesus Christ was born of a woman but without a contribution of the seed of a man but by the overshadowing of the Holy Spirit. Hence, though St Joseph was the foster father of Jesus Christ and the spouse of the Blessed Virgin Mary, the true Father of Christ Jesus is the Holy Spirit. The Spouse of Mary in the order of grace as regards the birth of Jesus Christ is also the Holy Spirit. Our new birth is of the Word and the Holy Spirit. "For you have been born anew, not of perishable but of imperishable seed, through the living and enduring word of God." – 1 Peter 1:23. Again, "Jesus answered, "Very truly, I tell you, no one can enter the kingdom of God without being born of water and Spirit. What is born of the flesh is flesh, and what is born of the Spirit is spirit. Do not be astonished that I said to you, 'You must be born from above." – John 3:5-7. Being born again by the same

Spouse of Mary through whom she gave birth to Jesus Christ, we are children of Mary.

This Jesus Christ is "the firstborn from the dead, that in all things He may have the pre-eminence." – Colossians 1:18b. In the book of Revelation, concerning Christ, it was also stated "Jesus Christ, the faithful witness, the firstborn from the dead, and the ruler over the kings of the earth." – Revelation 1:5.

How was Jesus Christ as "the firstborn from the dead" born? Jesus, speaking with Nicodemus said: "That which is born of the flesh is flesh, and that which is born of the Spirit is spirit." – John 3:6. In the gospel of Mathew it was written: "Now the birth of Jesus Christ was as follows: After His mother Mary was betrothed to Joseph, before they came together, she was found with child of the Holy Spirit." – Mathew 1:18. The birth of Jesus Christ as the firstborn from the dead is of the same Spirit that overshadowed Mary for him to be born in flesh thus: "But if the Spirit of Him who raised Jesus from the dead dwells in you, He who raised Christ from the dead will also give life to your mortal bodies through His Spirit who dwells in you." – Romans 8:11

Once again, brethren, there is a mystery here that needs to be unravelled. When the Holy Spirit incarnated Jesus Christ in the womb of Mary, you were also incarnated therein. You were in Jesus Christ while He was in the womb of Mary. This is to say that all Christians, not just only the Christians but the entire human race were actually in Christ while He was in the womb of Mary. The scripture revealed: "For if we have been united together in the likeness of His death, certainly we also shall be in the likeness of His resurrection, knowing this, that our old man was crucified with Him, that the body of sin might be done away with, that we should no longer be slaves of sin. For he who has died has been freed from sin. Now if we died with Christ, we believe that we shall also live with

Him, knowing that Christ, having been raised from the dead, dies no more. Death no longer has dominion over Him." – Romans 6:5-9. It was because we were in Christ even while in the womb of Mary that we were able to die with him when he died. The entire human race is the children of Mary, but Christians are her children in a particular way.

As a new creation, Christians are born of the same Spirit which overshadowed Mary, and she conceived of Jesus. Mary never stops being the mother of Jesus Christ, being his mother by the Eternal Holy Spirit. As we were in Christ at his birth, life, death and resurrection, we are still in Christ Jesus as He is seated at the Father's right-hand side. We are seated together with Him (see Ephesians 2:6). Again, "Whoever is united with the Lord is one with him in spirit." – 1 Corinthians 6:17.

Moreover, the scripture revealed that "Christ is the head of the church, his body, of which he is the Saviour." – Ephesians 5:23b. In Colossians one verse eighteen it is also revealed thus: "And he (Christ Jesus) is the head of the body, the church; he is the beginning and the firstborn from among the dead, so that in everything he might have the supremacy." The head and the body cannot have different mothers but one. As such, the mother of Christ, the head, is also the mother of his body, the church. Hence, Mary is our mother as the member of this Church that is His Body.

The Church elaborated further on the motherhood of Mary thus:

"Mary's function as mother of men in no way obscures or diminishes this unique mediation of Christ, but rather shows its power. But the Blessed Virgin's salutary influence on men . . . flows forth from the superabundance of the merits of Christ, rests on his mediation, depends entirely on it and draws all its power from it.' 'No creature could ever be counted along with the Incarnate Word and Redeemer; but just as the priesthood of Christ is shared in various ways both by his ministers and the faithful, and as the one goodness of God is radiated in different ways among his creatures, so also the unique mediation of the Redeemer does not exclude but rather gives rise to a manifold co-operation which is but a sharing in this one source.'" (CCC), 1994, para 970.

The scripture reveals to us that Mary has never stopped being the mother of Jesus Christ. The same scripture and the teachings of the Church reveal to us that Mary is our mother by God's grace and will. Mary is both the Lioness of Judah and the Sheep that gave birth to the Lamb.

Mary is the Lioness and the Sheep

As the lioness gives birth to a lion, a sheep gives birth to a lamb. Jesus Christ is the Lion and the Lamb. Hence, Mary, the mother of Jesus Christ is the Lioness and the Sheep. The apostle John heard "a loud voice: 'Worthy is the Lamb who was slain To receive power and riches and wisdom, And strength and honour and glory and blessing!'" – Revelation 5:12. It is also written: "All who dwell on the earth will worship him, whose names have not been written in the Book of Life of the Lamb slain from the foundation of the world." – Revelation 13:8. This Lamb of the sacrifice must be born by a Sheep. God can do all things. The Lamb does not have to be born but in God's almightiness, He had willed that His Lamb must be born. When we see a lamb, we are to ask where the sheep that gave birth to it is.

Once again, apostle John in his vision wept so much. Why? "Because no one was found worthy to open and read the scroll, or to look at it. But one of the elders said to me, "Do not weep. Behold, the Lion of the tribe of Judah, the Root of David, has prevailed to open the scroll and to loose its seven seals." And I looked, and behold, in the midst of the throne and of the four living creatures, and in the midst of the elders, stood a Lamb as though it had been slain, having seven horns and seven eyes, which are the seven Spirits of God sent out into all the earth. Then He came and took the scroll out of the right hand of Him who sat on the throne."

We marvel at the sight of this Sheep that is so privileged by the Almighty God to be favoured to be the Mother of the Lamb. This worthy Lamb is so interconnected with the Sheep that gave birth to Him even in His self-sacrifice sacrificed before the foundation of the world because the scripture revealed this to us thus: "Simeon blessed them and said to Mary, his mother: "This child is destined to cause the falling and rising of many in Israel, and to be a sign that will be spoken against, so that the thoughts of many hearts will be revealed. And a sword will pierce your own soul too." – Luke 2:34-35. When the scripture says "a sword will pierce your own soul too" it means that that sword had pierced a soul, which of course is the soul of Jesus Christ, the Lamb and will pierce Mary's soul too.

How can you ignore this woman that the sword which pierced the soul of Jesus Christ pierced her soul too? How can you not honour and respect such a woman? Always remember that she was singularly honoured and favoured by the Almighty Father.

Honour and Respect God's Choice

God chooses different people for various purposes. It is not a matter of who they are or what they have done. It is simply the divine choice. Who can question God? Can a pot question the potter? He chose Abram who later He called Abraham for a purpose, and we honour and respect him as our father in faith. God chose Moses, not because Moses was worthy of being chosen but simply because it was God's choice. While choosing Moses God said: "Come now, therefore, and I will send you to Pharaoh that you may bring My people, the children of Israel, out of Egypt." – Exodus 3:10. Moses, aware of his unworthiness answered God: "But Moses said to God, "Who am I that I should go to Pharaoh, and that I should bring the children of Israel out of Egypt?" – vs 11. Again, Moses pointed out another shortcoming of his thus: "O my Lord, I am not eloquent, neither before nor since You have spoken to Your servant; but I am slow of speech and slow of tongue." – Exodus 4:10. God has made up His mind in his choice and nothing can stop Him. You can also stop excusing yourself as to why God cannot use you. In Christ Jesus you are also a chosen of the Lord, all your shortcomings notwithstanding. We honour and respect Moses. The law given to Moses by God is called the law of Moses.

In the same way, when God chose Mary: "Then the angel said to her, "Do not be afraid, Mary, for you have found favour with God. And behold, you will conceive in your womb and bring forth a Son, and shall call His name Jesus. He will be great, and will be called the Son of the Highest; and the Lord God will give Him the throne of His father David. And He will reign over the house of Jacob forever, and of His kingdom, there will be no end." – Luke 1:30-33. Mary, also realising her shortcoming said to the angel: "How can this be, since I do not know a man?" – vs 34.

Concerning the shortcomings of Moses: "So the Lord said to him, "Who has made man's mouth? Or who makes the mute, the deaf, the seeing, or the blind? Have not I, the Lord? Now therefore, go, and I will be with your mouth and teach you what you shall say." – Exodus 4:11-12. The Lord through His angel also answered Mary regarding the shortcoming that she pointed out: "And the angel answered and said to her, "The Holy Spirit will come upon you, and the power of the Highest will overshadow you; therefore, also, that Holy One who is to be born will be called the Son of God." - Luke 1:35. We should also honour and respect Mary, who is God's choice. She played an indispensable role in the economy of our salvation.

Speaking Against God's Choice
There is a temptation to disrespect, grumble, murmur, and complain against God's choice. There is usually negative consequence in standing against God's chosen. The scripture revealed: "Whoever listens to you listens to me, and whoever rejects you rejects me, and whoever rejects me rejects the one who sent me." – Luke 10:16. "Miriam and Aaron spoke against Moses ... So, they said, "Has the Lord indeed spoken only through Moses? Has He not spoken through us also?" And the Lord heard it. (Now the man Moses was very humble, more than all men who were on the face of the earth.)." – Numbers 12:1-3. God was unhappy that they spoke against

His servant Moses: "So the anger of the Lord was aroused against them, and He departed. And when the cloud departed from above the tabernacle, suddenly Miriam became leprous, as white as snow. Then Aaron turned toward Miriam, and there she was, a leper. So, Aaron said to Moses, "Oh, my lord! Please do not lay this sin on us, in which we have done foolishly and in which we have sinned. Please do not let her be as one dead, whose flesh is half consumed when he comes out of his mother's womb!" So, Moses cried out to the Lord, saying, "Please heal her, O God, I pray!" – Numbers 12:9-13.

The scripture warned: "Do not touch my anointed ones; do my prophets no harm." – Psalm 105:15. Do not speak against God's chosen ones. Do not speak against Mary, the mother, the nurse, the nurturer and the greatest and longest companion of the Lord, Jesus Christ.

Imagine this Lady going about her daily duties, fully aware of who she was carrying. When Joseph was making plans to divorce her secretly, she did not protest. She was resigned to the will of God: "Then Mary said, "Behold the maidservant of the Lord! Let it be to me according to your word." – Luke 1:38. If Moses was so humble, imagine the humility of this Lady.

Having spoken against Mary and you did not become leprous like Marriam does not imply that God approves your deeds. Grace and mercy have come to us through Jesus Christ. "For the Law was given through Moses, but grace [the unearned, undeserved favour of God] and truth came through Jesus Christ." – John 1:17 (AMP). God is constantly being patient with us and giving us opportunities to know the truth: the truth about Him, His chosen ones and the truth about you.

The Lion roars and remains the King of kings. The Lioness roars in unison with the Lion in a subtle but powerful way. Let us listen and honour her.

The Power of the Roaring Voice of the Lioness

The Lion of Judah is the Word. "In the beginning was the Word: the Word was with God and the Word was God."- John 1:1. The Word was made flesh (i.e. became a human being), he lived among us. . ." – John 1:14. Mary is the mother of this Word. It is in and through her that the Word became a human being to dwell among us.

The scripture did not record many of Mary's activities purposefully. She is a Secret Garden where the Son of God took repose for thirty years. The Eternal Father waited for her "yes" for the Word to incarnate in her womb. Other times that she spoke, there was divine manifestation or intervention.

God acts whenever Mary, the Lioness of Judah speaks. Having been told of Elizabeth's pregnancy by the angel, Mary set out to visit her. The scripture recorded the visit thus: "At that time Mary got ready and hurried to a town in the hill country of Judea, where she entered Zechariah's home and greeted Elizabeth. When Elizabeth heard Mary's greeting, the baby leaped in her womb, and Elizabeth was filled with the Holy Spirit." – Luke 1:39-41. Elizabeth hearing the voice of Mary, the baby in her womb (John the Baptist) leapt for joy in her womb. Elizabeth could perceive it, and she declared it. Again, she was filled with the Holy Spirit by merely hearing the roaring of the Lioness of Judah, Mary's greeting. She could not control herself under the power of the Holy Spirit and with a loud voice, she began to declare what was revealed to her by the Holy Spirit about Mary. It is not surprising that

Elizabeth had this encounter. The Holy Spirit overshadowed Mary and the Word incarnate was dwelling in her womb. Imagine what will happen now that she is dwelling in the realm of glory!

Again, the Lioness of Judah was with the Lion of Judah at the wedding feast at Cana in Galilee. When she roared, the divine Kairos regarding the time for Jesus Christ to start His ministry of working miracles and signs instantly changed. Jesus Christ made it clear that His time of working miracles had not yet come. Mary insisted that the miracle had to be performed, the timing notwithstanding for many reasons later stated. Jesus could neither resist nor refuse her. Her voice, though subtle, is powerful when she roars! I would like you to know that there is a union beyond human comprehension, far beyond what is revealed in the scriptures that exist between Mary, the Lioness of Judah and the Eternal Father, the Eternal Son and the Holy Spirit (see John 21:25). The Lioness roared in the spirit on the Pentecost Day after the descent of the Holy Spirit. How then can you not respect and honour Mary because you are Charismatic or Pentecostal?

Lioness of Judah Spoke in Tongues

The scripture recorded the Pentecost Day experience thus: "Then the apostles returned to Jerusalem from the hill called the Mount of Olives, a Sabbath day's walk from the city. . . . They all joined together constantly in prayer, along with the women **and Mary the mother of Jesus**, and with his brothers. . . . . When the day of Pentecost came, they were all together in one place. . . . They saw what seemed to be tongues of fire that separated and came to rest on each of them. **All of them were filled with the Holy Spirit and began to speak in other tongues as the Spirit enabled them**." – Acts 1:12, 14; 2:1, 3-4. (emphasis added).

The Lioness of Judah was there in the Upper Room and waited for the descent of the Holy Spirit with the other 119 disciples (Acts 1:15) of Jesus Christ. She also spoke in tongues and those who came to celebrate Pentecost heard her in their native language praising God. She was among those mistaken for drunkards (Acts 2:13). She also praised Him (but in the vernacular) when she was at her cousin Elizabeth's house, declaring the great marvels God had done.

We are showing you that those who were the foundations of the Church were with Mary. You that is built on this foundation, how can you despise her? Those who were filled with the Holy Spirit and were the first to speak in tongues were with her and she spoke in tongues with them. How can you despise her because you are full of the Holy Spirit, and you are speaking in tongues?

Remember that she was so overshadowed by the Holy Spirit that the Word became incarnate in her by the power of the Holy Spirit. She carried the incarnate Word in her womb for nine months so that He may be born so that He may die to set you free. This shows that the Eternal Father incorporated her to play a very significant role in the economy of our salvation.

The Holy Spirit, the Helper that has come to dwell with us and in us forever is her Spouse. He was responsible for the incarnation of our Lord Jesus Christ in her womb. As people filled with the Holy Spirit, we are supposed to show her lots of honour and respect. God reveals His plan for us through Mary.

The Mirror of the Divine Plan

In the scriptures, the Lord revealed his plan for humanity. God said: "They will know that I am the Lord their God, who brought them out of Egypt so that I might dwell among them. I am the Lord their God." Through His prophet, he said: "My dwelling place will be with them; I will be their God, and they will be my people. Then the nations will know that I the Lord make Israel holy, when my sanctuary is among them forever" – Ezekiel 37:27-28. Mary became the Ark of Covenant hosting the Incarnate Word who is also the Temple that will and was rebuilt in three days when destroyed.

Concerning the sanctuary, God thus commanded Moses: "Then have them make a sanctuary for me, and I will dwell among them. Make this tabernacle and all its furnishings exactly like the pattern I will show you." – Exodus 25:8-9. We know that these are foreshadows of the things to come. The Lord through prophet Isiah revealed: "The virgin will conceive and give birth to a son, and will call him Immanuel (meaning God with us)." – Isiah 7:14b.

Mary is the mirror of God's plan for us. God dwelt in her for nine months to be born for our salvation. For those of us who believe in Jesus Christ, he has given us the privilege to become children of God now in this world (1 John 3:2). He has given us the gift of salvation, righteousness and eternal life. He has made us His temples to become His habitation, His temples here on earth. The Spirit through St Paul revealed: "For we are the temple of the living God. As God has said: "I will live with them and walk among them, and I will be their God, and they will be my people." – 2 Corinthians 6:16.

For the born-again Christians, Jesus is more than Immanuel. He is not just the God that is dwelling among us, He has become the God that is in us. Mary, the mother of Jesus Christ, is the mirror of this God's plan because as God was incarnated in her and dwelt within her for nine months, He is now dwelling in us in His resurrected person, by the Holy Spirit. Jesus revealed that we are to become God-carriers like Mary if we believe and accept the Word as Mary did. Concerning this Jesus said: "Who is my mother, and who are my brothers?" Pointing to his disciples, he said, "Here are my mother and my brothers. For whoever does the will of my Father in heaven is my brother and sister and mother." – Mathew 12:48-50. The Spirit later said: "Do you not know that your bodies are temples of the Holy Spirit, who is in you, whom you have received from God? You are not your own." – 1 Corinthians 6:19.

Jesus Christ is the firstborn of the dead about His resurrection. We are to follow as His brothers and sisters. We can also rightly say that Mary is the first of the God-carriers. In union with her, we are also presently God-carriers. Hence, mothers of Jesus Christ by the divine order as revealed by Jesus Christ.

The Word of God is the mirror in which we see ourselves. For it is written: "But we all, with unveiled face, beholding as in a mirror the glory of the Lord, are being transformed into the same image from glory to glory, just as by the Spirit of the Lord." – 2 Corinthians 3:18. St James went further to tell us about this mirror thus: "But be doers of the word, and not hearers only, deceiving yourselves. For if anyone is a hearer of the word and not a doer, he is like a man observing his natural face in a mirror; for he observes himself, goes away, and immediately forgets what kind of man he was. But he who looks into the perfect law of liberty and continues in it, and is not a forgetful hearer but a doer of the work, this one will be blessed in what he does." – James 1:22-25.

Mary is Jesus' mother not just because she was a highly favoured, chosen one but also because she was a doer of the Word. As a born-again child of God, you have also been chosen by God. Scripture reveals this thus: "But you are a chosen generation, a royal priesthood, a holy nation, His own special people, that you may proclaim the praises of Him who called you out of darkness into His marvellous light." – 1 Peter 2:9.

Behold, God has also highly favoured you. He made you His own righteousness (2 Corinthians 5:21). He chose you and separated you from the world so that though you are in the world, you are not of the world. He has made you His peculiar person, a new kind of species that has been capacitated to share in his divine nature. He did all these not because you are worthy or because of anything you have done but simply because He wants to. All He now requires of you to become the mother of His Son like Mary is as you hear the Word to believe and do whatever the Word tells you. This Word that is our mirror incarnated in Mary. We have to know that as He dwelt within her in His incarnation, He is dwelling with her more gloriously presently. For the children of God, Mary is the revelation of the fulfilment of God's plan.

Beholding the motherhood of Mary, we can affirm that indeed there is nothing impossible with God. Beholding Mary and Jesus Christ, you can marvel at what God has made you to become. Human senses cannot perceive it. Human understanding cannot comprehend it. Human philosophy and all other human disciplines cannot capture it; they may only have a glimpse of this marvel. You must receive it by revelation and believe it. "As Jesus was saying these things, a woman in the crowd called out, "Blessed is the mother who gave you birth and nursed you." He replied, "Blessed rather are those who hear the word of God and obey it." – Luke 11:27-28. Once again, Jesus by answering the woman in the crowd revealed how Mary became His mother and how you too can become blessed and His mother too. Mary is indeed the mother of God!

Theotokos the Mother of the Lion of Judah

The Virgin Mary became the mirror showing us what it is like to have the indwelling of God within us. For the Word to become flesh and to dwell among us, He had to first dwell in the womb of the virgin as prophesied: "Therefore the Lord Himself will give you a sign: Listen carefully, the virgin will conceive and give birth to a son, and she will call his name Immanuel (God with us)." – Isaiah 7:14 (AMP). Prophet Isaiah further prophesied concerning Him thus: "For to us a Child shall be born, to us a Son shall be given; and the government shall be upon His shoulder, and His name shall be called Wonderful Counsellor, Mighty God, Everlasting Father, Prince of Peace. There shall be no end to the increase of His government and of peace, [He shall rule] on the throne of David and over his kingdom, to establish it and to uphold it with justice and righteousness from that time forward and forevermore. The zeal of the Lord of hosts will accomplish this." – Isaiah 9: 6-7 (AMP). The scripture reveals to us that this Woman is indeed the mother of God. How can we not reverence and honour her as such?

The Holy Spirit through the apostle John who took Mary home from the Golgotha after Christ's crucifixion gave us this revelation: "In the beginning was the Word, and the Word was with God, and the Word was God. He was with God in the beginning. Through him all things were made; without him, nothing was made that has been made. The Word became flesh and made his dwelling among us. We have seen his glory, the glory of the one and only Son, who came from the Father, full of grace and truth." – John 1:1-3, 14. For the Word to become flesh and dwell among us, He dwelt in the womb of the Virgin Mary from whence He took flesh to dwell among us to accomplish the work of our salvation. Having been glorified, similar to dwelling in the womb of the Blessed Virgin, He is now to dwell within us. It was thus revealed: "Behold, I stand at the door, and knock: if any man hears my voice, and open the door, I will come into him, and will sup with him, and he with me." – Revelation 3:20. Again, in John 14:23 the Spirit gave us this revelation: "Jesus answered and said unto him, If a man loves me, he will keep my words: and my Father will love him, and we will come unto him, and make our abode with him." It is then not surprising for Jesus to give this revelation in the gospel of Mathew when he said: "But he answered and said unto him that told him, Who is my mother? and who are my brethren? And he stretched forth his hand toward his disciples, and said, Behold my mother and my brethren! For whosoever shall do the will of my Father which is in heaven, the same is my brother, and sister, and mother." – Mathew 12:48-50.

    We see this same Jesus, the Son of God, the Lion of Judah resurrected in glory with the same body incarnated through the womb of Mary. After his resurrection, he said: "Behold My hands and My feet, that it is I Myself. Handle Me and see, for a spirit does not have flesh and bones as you see I have." When He had said this, He showed them His hands and His feet. But while they still did not believe for joy, and marvelled, He said to them, "Have you any food here?" So they gave Him a piece of a broiled fish and some honeycomb. And He took it and ate in their presence." – Luke 24:39-43. While Jesus was seated in glory, the Spirit revealed him to St. Stephen thus: "But Stephen, full of the Holy Spirit, looked up to heaven and saw the glory of God, and Jesus standing at the right hand of God. "Look," he said, "I see heaven open and the Son of Man standing at the right hand of God." – Acts 7:55-56. Behold the incarnated body of Jesus Christ, the Lion of Judah, taken of the Lioness of Judah, glorified!

The Spirit showed us the glory and the glorified body of Jesus Christ in greater detail through the revelation He gave to the apostle John. This descriptive revelation was given to us thus: "On the Lord's Day I was in the Spirit, and I heard behind me a loud voice like a trumpet . . . I turned around to see the voice that was speaking to me. And when I turned, I saw seven golden lampstands, and among the lampstands was someone like a son of man, dressed in a robe reaching down to his feet and with a golden sash around his chest. The hair on his head was white like wool, as white as snow, and his eyes were like blazing fire. His feet were like bronze glowing in a furnace, and his voice was like the sound of rushing waters. In his right hand he held seven stars, and coming out of his mouth was a sharp, double-edged sword. His face was like the sun shining in all its brilliance. When I saw him, I fell at his feet as though dead. Then he placed his right hand on me and said: "Do not be afraid. I am the First and the Last. I am the Living One; I was dead, and now look, I am alive for ever and ever! And I hold the keys of death and Hades." – Revelation 1:10, 12-18. Alleluia! Alleluia!

Remember that this is the same Jesus that John was leaning on his chest during the Last Supper. This is the same Jesus that John was with for over three years. He walked with him, ate with him, and lived in the same house with him. Yet, seeing him in his glory, John fell face down as dead. The body of Jesus glorified is the body he took from the Blessed Mary. Do you suppose such a Woman He took her body unglorified? You need to remember that Jesus enjoyed an inseparable union with Mary here on earth. It has not changed after His glorification.

Inseparable Union of Jesus and Mary

A sword will pierce Jesus Christ's soul.
The same sword pierced the Virgin Mary's soul.

Oh, a revelation of an inseparable union!
Oh, a revelation of a co-victimhood union!
Son of Man took the body of the Virgin Mary.

Any time we meditate on the humanity of Jesus,
We should not ignore Mary.
Son of Man took the body of the Virgin Mary.

Any time we behold the Cross of our salvation,
We should not ignore Mary.
Son of Man took the body of the Virgin Mary.

Any time we behold that resurrected body with wounds,
We should not ignore Mary.
Son of Man took the body of the Virgin Mary.

Any time we hold and raise that Communion Bread,
We should not ignore Mary.
Son of Man took the body of the Virgin Mary.

Any time we hold and raise that Communion Chalice,
We should not ignore Mary.
Son of Man took the body of the Virgin Mary.

Behold the scare of the sword on the soul of Jesus!
Behold too the scare of the same sword on the soul of Mary!

Beholding these scares,
We should not ignore Mary.

The lowly handmaid of the Lord is Mary,
But behold what the Lord has done for Mary.
The Lord who raises the lowly!
The Lord who casts down the proud from thrones!

Among all women most blessed!
All generations must call her Blessed!
This generation must call her Blessed!
My family and I must call her Blessed!

Your family and you must call her Blessed!
Mary, so highly favoured, is indeed Blessed!

Thinking of the Lion of the tribe of Judah,
We must think of and honour the Lioness of the tribe of Judah.

Thinking of the Lamb that was slain,
We must think of and honour the Sheep that was also pierced.

This "Woman" is the mirror of the divine plan for humanity:
"We are the temple of the living God."
"I will live with them and walk among them."
"I will be their God, and they will be my people."

As this "Woman" was favoured to be the God-carrier,
All humans, "Born-again," are now the God-carriers.

Oh, Mary, the pride and glory of the womanhood!
Oh, Mary, the pride and glory of the human race!

Gifted to the dark, hopeless world,
Within her dwelt the Light and the Hope of the world.

Behold the Word that created all in the world,
In the world chose this creature to be birthed for the world.
Oh, we're fearfully and wonderfully made,

To birth the Word for the world.

In the dark of the night birthed the Light of the world.
To the manger draws the lowlys and majesties of the world.

The Lion of the tribe of Judah loudly roars!
The Lioness of the tribe of Judah mildly roars!
Do whatever He tells you, she mildly roars.
"As He is, so are we in this world;" we roar

Mary Must Respond for the Word to Incarnate

Mary exemplified that we need to respond to God's word as an active demonstration of our faith for God's intended purpose, miracles, signs and wonders to happen. She also went further to reveal to us that we need to make declarations of who God says that we are, God's purpose for our lives, works, marvels and the promises of God.

The Holy Spirit revealed what happened later: "It is written: "I believed; therefore, I have spoken." Since we have that same spirit of faith, we also believe and therefore speak." – 2 Corinthians 4:13. Angel Gabriel brought God's word to Mary that she was to be the mother of God as a virgin. As humanly impossible as it was, for the incarnation to occur, Mary must believe God. If she truly believed God in her heart, she must speak it out. The scripture revealed this divine principle for manifestation of the impossible when as it is written: "For with the heart one believes unto righteousness, and with the mouth confession is made unto salvation." – Romans 10:10. It means that if you believe God's word, you must confess it with your mouth for the miracle to take place. This is the reason Mary had to respond to the word. You can recall the call of the prophet Samuel. When God was calling him, until he responded to God, God never spoke to him (see 1 Samuel 1:1-10). It means that we must respond to God for divine interventions to occur. We will come to that later but at the moment let us focus on Mary's response to the word and her declarations.

In the Gospel of Luke chapter one, from verse twenty-six, the angel greeted Mary and delivered an incredible message of the Eternal Father's intention for the Word to become Incarnate and to make Mary the mother of His Word Incarnate. She questioned the angel thus: "How can this be, since I do not know a man?" The angel explained the role of the Holy Spirit in bringing about her intended pregnancy with the Word Incarnate. Mary had to respond. She responded thus: "Behold the maidservant of the Lord! Let it be to me according to your word."

Mary's response sealed the divine deal. Instantly, she became pregnant of the Word by the overshadowing power of the Holy Spirit. When Elizabeth, her cousin, by the same power of the Holy Spirit received the revelation of what the Lord had done for Mary and the world, she marvelled at her privilege to be visited by Mary. Mary responded with declarations by saying:

"My soul magnifies the Lord,
And my spirit has rejoiced in God my Savior.
For He has regarded the lowly state of His maidservant.
For behold, henceforth all generations will call me blessed.
For He who is mighty has done great things for me,
And holy is His name.
And His mercy is on those who fear Him
From generation to generation.
He has shown strength with His arm.
He has scattered the proud in the imagination of their hearts.
He has put down the mighty from their thrones,
And exalted the lowly.
He has filled the hungry with good things,
And the rich He has sent away empty.

He has helped His servant Israel,
In remembrance of His mercy,
As He spoke to our fathers,
To Abraham and to his seed forever."[5]

God is in a relationship with humans. Yes, God the Father, Son and the Holy Spirit wants you to be in a relationship with Him. Otherwise, there will be no need for the Word to become flesh and be as we are, tempted in every way but without sin. There will be no need for Jesus to be the Son of Mary and Joseph. All these happen because God wants to be in a relationship with you. When He speaks to you through His word, the Bible, and other means He also expects you to respond. It is highly exemplified also in the right of baptism and other sacraments. For you to become born again, it is not enough to believe in your heart, you must confess from your mouth too. As such, for you to receive your miracles, signs and wonders, you must believe in your heart but must also confess with you mouth. We can see the example in Mary's interaction with Archangel Gabriel.

---

[5] Luke 1:46-55

Imitate Mary in Response and Declaration of the Word

The Spirit says: "The word is near you, in your mouth and in your heart" (that is, the word of faith which we preach): that if you confess with your mouth the Lord Jesus and believe in your heart that God has raised Him from the dead, you will be saved." – Romans 10:8-9. The Word must be in your heart and mouth, and you have to speak it.

Jesus being told of His family waiting outside to see Him asked: "Who is My mother and who are My brothers?" And He stretched out His hand toward His disciples and said, "Here are My mother and My brothers! For whoever does the will of My Father in heaven is My brother and sister and mother." – Mathew 12:48-50. Mary is the mother of Jesus Christ. Jesus then revealed to us that we too can also become his mother by also doing the will of the Father as Mary did. One of the wills of the Father in this instance is for us to respond to the Word when we hear it. The Spirit, in the book of Romans, revealed that when we hear the word and believe it, we must declare that word for supernatural manifestation and salvation. Hence, "If you confess with your mouth the Lord Jesus and believe in your heart that God has raised Him from the dead, you will be saved. For with the heart, one believes unto righteousness, and with the mouth, confession is made unto salvation." – Romans 10:9-10.

The scripture declared that faith without work is dead. The major and most important work of faith is speaking. If you believe it, you declare it to yourself and unto God. Mary was alone with the angel Gabriel when the message of the Father was given to her. When she believed the angel, immediately, responded.

However, you must be very careful what you declare when you hear from God. "False humility" of self-degradation is very dangerous and deadly. The example of a dangerous and deadly confession can be seen in the response of many Israelis when the spies gave negative and "factual" reports of the land they spied on. There are twelve of them who spied on the land. Two of them remembered the promise of God and believed that what they saw notwithstanding, they could take possession of the land. However, the ten of them forgot the promise of God to the patriarchs and could not believe that they could take possession of the land and confessed it.

Two of the twelve spies, Joshua and Caleb, who believed God declared: "We should go up and take possession of the land, for we can certainly do it." Furthermore, "The land we passed through and explored is exceedingly good. If the Lord is pleased with us, he will lead us into that land, a land flowing with milk and honey, and will give it to us. Only do not rebel against the Lord. And do not be afraid of the people of the land, because we will devour them. Their protection is gone, but the Lord is with us. Do not be afraid of them." – Numbers 14:7-9. It was revealed later in the passage that Joshua and Caleb received the land per their confessions.

On the other hand, the other ten spies gave a different report and confession. They said: "We can't attack those people; they are stronger than we are." And they spread among the Israelites a bad report about the land they had explored. They said, "The land we explored devours those living in it. All the people we saw there are of great size. We saw the Nephilim there (the descendants of Anak come from the Nephilim). We seemed like grasshoppers in our own eyes, and we looked the same to them." – Numbers 13:31-33. The community believed them and wept and wished they would go back to bondage in Egypt. By their words, those who grumbled and confessed lack of faith in the work and promises of God did not enter the promised land by their words. Scripture revealed that it is by our words we are condemned and by our words we are justified (see Matthew 12:37). God wants us to control our words by controlling our thoughts. We need to be careful what we believe and what we confess. Hence, he counselled us to guard our hearts with all diligence because out it is the issue of life (Proverbs 4:23). Again, "Death and life are in the power of the tongue, and those who love it will eat its fruit." – Proverbs 18:21. Joshua and Caleb got life and the other ten spies and those who confess in unison with them got death.

Scripture further told us that we should uphold our faith in God and His words to us when King Jehoshaphat said: "Listen to me, Judah and people of Jerusalem! Have faith in the Lord your God and you will be upheld; have faith in his prophets and you will be successful." – 2 Chronicles 20:20. It is as if the scripture is saying to us that we should believe God no matter how impossible it may seem. Looking at all that God has done; we believe Him and are upheld. We are to have faith in his word spoken to us through the scripture and we will be successful. The Amplified Version put it this way: "Hear me, O Judah, and you inhabitants of Jerusalem! Believe and trust in the Lord your God and you will be established (secure). Believe and trust in His prophets and succeed." Again, concerning listening to the word and speaking, God spoke to Joshua after the death of Moses thus: "Be strong and very courageous. Be careful to obey all the law my servant Moses gave you; do not turn from it to the right or to the left, that you may be successful wherever you go. **Keep this Book of the Law always on your lips; meditate on it day and night**, so that you may be careful to do everything written in it. Then you will be prosperous and successful." – Joshua 1:7-8 (emphases is added). God wants us to hear the word, meditate it in our hearts, believe it and speak it for the manifestation to occur. Following these directives of the Spirit helps us to know God. The Holy Spirit through prophet Hosea declared that His people are destroyed for lack of knowledge (see Hosea 4:6). Mary knows God.

Mary's Knowledge of Jesus Christ

Mary's knowledge of Jesus Christ is pure; it stems directly from God via revelation. Eternal Father sent the Archangel Gabriel to deliver a message concerning the incarnation of the Word to Mary. The angel was delivering a message that came directly from God. It was recorded thus:

"In the sixth month the angel Gabriel was sent by God to a town in Galilee called Nazareth, to a virgin engaged to a man whose name was Joseph, of the house of David. The virgin's name was Mary. And he came to her and said, "Greetings, favoured one! The Lord is with you." But she was much perplexed by his words and pondered what sort of greeting this might be. The angel said to her, "Do not be afraid, Mary, for you have found favour with God. And now, you will conceive in your womb and bear a son, and you will name him Jesus. He will be great, and will be called the Son of the Most High, and the Lord God will give to him the throne of his ancestor David. He will reign over the house of Jacob forever, and of his kingdom there will be no end." Mary said to the angel, "How can this be, since I am a virgin?" The angel said to her, "The Holy Spirit will come upon you, and the power of the Most High will overshadow you; therefore, the child to be born will be holy; he will be called Son of God. And now, your relative Elizabeth in her old age has also conceived a son; and this is the sixth month for her who was said to be barren. For nothing will be impossible with God." Then Mary said, "Here am I, the servant of the Lord; let it be with me according to your word." Then the angel departed from her." – Luke 1:26-38

This scriptural record revealed that from the very beginning, Mary received the revelation of who Jesus, the Son she was to conceive, was. She knew He is the Son of God ("He will be called Son of God"). She knew He was the promised Messiah ("the Lord God will give to him the throne of his ancestor David"). She knew that He is not of the seed of man but of the power of the Holy Spirit ("The Holy Spirit will come upon you, and the power of the Most High will overshadow you; therefore, the child to be born will be holy; he will be called Son of God."). When Jesus was conceived of Mary no one else in this world knew who Jesus was except her, not even Joseph, her betrothed.

Joseph's knowledge of Jesus also came through revelation as the scripture recorded: "Now the birth of Jesus the Messiah took place in this way. When his mother Mary had been engaged to Joseph, but before they lived together, she was found to be with child from the Holy Spirit. Her husband Joseph, being a righteous man and unwilling to expose her to public disgrace, planned to dismiss her quietly. But just when he had resolved to do this, an angel of the Lord appeared to him in a dream and said, "Joseph, son of David, do not be afraid to take Mary as your wife, for the child conceived in her is from the Holy Spirit. She will bear a son, and you are to name him Jesus, for he will save his people from their sins." – Matthew 1:18-21. The revelation that Joseph received in the person of Jesus Christ became a confirmation to Mary of the message she got from the visitation of the angel. Of course, she was never in doubt.

Furthermore, when Mary visited her cousin Elizabeth, the message of the angel Gabriel was further proven to be true. First, she found Elizabeth to be truly six months pregnant. Lastly, the Holy Spirit gave Elizabeth revelation of Mary's pregnancy and about who she was carrying in her womb thus: "In those days Mary set out and went with haste to a Judean town in the hill country, where she entered the house of Zechariah and greeted Elizabeth. When Elizabeth heard Mary's greeting, the child leaped in her womb. And Elizabeth was filled with the Holy Spirit and exclaimed with a loud cry, "Blessed are you among women, and blessed is the fruit of your womb. And why has this happened to me, that the mother of my Lord comes to me? For as soon as I heard the sound of your greeting, the child in my womb leaped for joy. And blessed is she who believed that there would be a fulfilment of what was spoken to her by the Lord." – Luke 1:39-45. The revelation given to Elizabeth by the Holy Spirit confirmed to Mary the message of the Eternal Father through the angel Gabriel.

The shepherds who were watching over their flocks at night when Jesus was born received a revelation that they also shared with Mary and Joseph. It was thus revealed: "In that region there were shepherds living in the fields, keeping watch over their flock by night. Then an angel of the Lord stood before them, and the glory of the Lord shone around them, and they were terrified. But the angel said to them, "Do not be afraid; for see—I am bringing you good news of great joy for all the people: to you is born this day in the city of David a Savior, who is the Messiah, the Lord. This will be a sign for you: you will find a child wrapped in bands of cloth and lying in a manger." And suddenly there was with the angel a multitude of the heavenly host, praising God and saying, "Glory to God in the highest heaven, and on earth peace among those whom he favours!" When the angels had left them and gone into heaven, the shepherds said to one another, "Let us go now to Bethlehem and see this thing that has taken place, which the Lord has made known to us." So, they went with haste and found Mary and Joseph, and the child lying in the manger. When they saw this, they made known what had been told them about this child; and all who heard it were amazed at what the shepherds told them. But Mary treasured all these words and pondered them in her heart. The shepherds returned, glorifying and praising God for all they had heard and seen, as it had been told them." Luke 2:8-20. Here we see the shepherds receiving a revelation of the person of Jesus Christ and Mary hearing of the revelation they received treasured them and pondered them in her heart.

Once again, when Mary and Joseph took Mary to the temple to present him to the Eternal Father, she received another revelation of the person of Jesus, His mission on earth and the manner of His death and how Mary will share in His salvific wounds. It was written thus: "Now there was a man in Jerusalem whose name was Simeon; this man was righteous and devout, looking forward to the consolation of Israel, and the Holy Spirit rested on him. It had been revealed to him by the Holy Spirit that he would not see death before he had seen the Lord's Messiah. Guided by the Spirit, Simeon came into the temple; and when the parents brought in the child Jesus, to do for him what was customary under the law, Simeon took him in his arms and praised God . . . Then Simeon blessed them and said to his mother Mary, "This child is destined for the falling and the rising of many in Israel, and to be a sign that will be opposed so that the inner thoughts of many will be revealed—and a sword will pierce your own soul too." – Luke 2:25-35

Mary's knowledge of the person of Jesus Christ and His mission was demonstrated when they were at the wedding at Cana in Galilee. As a result of the revelation Mary received of who Jesus Christ was, confirmed by the subsequent revelations received by Joseph and others, Mary knew that nothing was impossible for Jesus.

Hence, it was written: "There was a wedding in Cana of Galilee, and the mother of Jesus was there. Jesus and his disciples had also been invited to the wedding. When the wine gave out, the mother of Jesus said to him, "They have no wine." And Jesus said to her, "Woman, what concern is that to you and to me? My hour has not yet come." His mother said to the servants, "Do whatever he tells you." Now standing there were six stone water jars for the Jewish rites of purification, each holding twenty or thirty gallons. Jesus said to them, "Fill the jars with water." And they filled them up to the brim. He said to them, "Now draw some out, and take it to the chief steward." So, they took it. When the steward tasted the water that had become wine, and did not know where it came from (though the servants who had drawn the water knew), the steward called the bridegroom and said to him, "Everyone serves the good wine first, and then the inferior wine after the guests have become drunk. But you have kept the good wine until now." Jesus did this, the first of his signs, in Cana of Galilee, and revealed his glory; and his disciples believed in him." – John 2:1-11.

Jesus Christ honours and respects Mary, His mother, and never takes any of her words for granted. The Blessed Trinity valued and treasured her so much that she was fully involved in the incarnation, birth, private life, public life, death and resurrection of Jesus Christ. She was also involved in the life of His Mystical Body, the Church, through her presence during the descent of the Holy Spirit on the Pentecost day. Reverence her and call her blessed You will be fulfilling the scripture by doing so.

Mary and the Manifestation of the Invisible God

Here is the description of the Lion of Judah, the Son of the Lioness of Judah. "He is the image of the invisible God, the firstborn over all creation. For by Him all things were created that are in heaven and that are on earth, visible and invisible, whether thrones or dominions or principalities or powers. All things were created through Him and for Him. And He is before all things, and in Him all things consist. And He is the head of the body, the church, who is the beginning, the firstborn from the dead, that in all things He may have the preeminence." - Colossians 1:15-18. This is one of the descriptions of Him who was born of the Lioness of Judah. He is the One who dwelt in this Woman's womb for at least nine months. He lived on earth for at least 30 years with this Woman. What other honour, respect, and recognition do you expect Jesus to bestow on His mother?

In the book of Revelation, the Spirit gave us this revelation: "Now a great sign appeared in heaven: a woman clothed with the sun, with the moon under her feet, and on her head a garland of twelve stars. Then being with child, she cried out in labour and in pain to give birth." – Revelation 12:1-2. Here the Lioness is roaring as she was in birth pangs for your salvation. She deserves our honour and respect.

Isaiah talked about this birth thus: For to us a child is born, to us a son is given, and the government will be on his shoulders. And he will be called Wonderful Counsellor, Mighty God, Everlasting Father, Prince of Peace. Of the greatness of his government and peace there will be no end. He will reign on David's throne and over his kingdom, establishing and upholding it with justice and righteousness from that time on and forever. The zeal of the Lord Almighty will accomplish this." – Isaiah 9:6-7. Meditate for a moment on the person of this child that is born, on this son that is given unto us. What kind of mother will give birth to this kind of son? She has to be blessed and highly favoured. God, the Holy Spirit, by overshadowing Mary for the incarnation of this son elevated her beyond human understanding and description. Such a position that the Eternal Father placed Mary by making her the mother of this Son can only be better understood through revelation.

Of course, common sense, natural order and science reveal a lot about Mary. We have already discussed most of such revelations in the previous chapters such as the law of biogenesis and the places of honour accorded to the mothers of the dignitaries of this world, including your mother.

Glorification and Coronation of the Lioness of Judah

Holy Spirit speaking through Hannah, the mother of prophet Samuel revealed the character of the God that chose Mary to be the mother of His Son. Speaking of the Almighty God, the Most High, she said: "He raiseth up the poor out of the dust, and lifteth up the beggar from the dunghill, to set them among princes, and to make them inherit the throne of glory." – 1 Samuel 2:8.

Mary, a young virgin living in Nazareth, was unknown to the world around her but known to the Almighty God. Her life changed forever when "God sent the angel Gabriel to Nazareth, a town in Galilee, to a virgin pledged to be married to a man named Joseph, a descendant of David. The virgin's name was Mary. – Luke 1:26-27. Concerning this divine visitation, glorification and the subsequent coronation Mary said: "He has been mindful of the humble state of his servant. From now on all generations will call me blessed, for the Mighty One has done great things for me, holy is his name. His mercy extends to those who fear him, from generation to generation. He has performed mighty deeds with his arm; he has scattered those who are proud in their inmost thoughts. He has brought down rulers from their thrones but has lifted up the humble." – Luke 1:48-52.

God indeed brought down rulers from their thrones as revealed through the prophet Isaiah thus: "How you are fallen from heaven, O Lucifer, son of the morning! How you are cut down to the ground, you who weakened the nations! For you have said in your heart: 'I will ascend into heaven, I will exalt my throne above the stars of God; I will also sit on the mount of the congregation on the farthest sides of the north; I will ascend above the heights of the clouds, I will be like the Most High.' Yet you shall be brought down to Sheol, to the lowest depths of the Pit." – Isaiah 14:12-15. God, the Most High, "resists the proud". 1 Peter 5:5c.

However, "He gives grace to the humble". 1 Peter 5:5d. Hence, God looking upon the humility of His handmaiden, the Lioness of Judah, lifted her up to become the mother of His Son. God then caused her to be set among the princes (see Isaiah 9:6) and to inherit a throne of glory.

It was revealed thus: "I saw heaven standing open and there before me was a white horse, whose rider is called Faithful and True. . . . and his name is the Word of God. The armies of heaven were following him . . . He will rule . . . with an iron sceptre. . . . On his robe and on his thigh, he has this name written: king of kings and lord of lords." – Revelation 19:11-16. The Lion of Judah, the Son of the Lioness of Judah, is the King of kings and Lord of lords. Implicitly, by the law of biogenesis, the Lioness of Judah is the Queen of queens.

This biogenesis law applies to what was done for the brothers of Jesus Christ. The Spirit revealed what was done for the faithful in Christ Jesus thus: "And God raised us up with Christ and seated us with him in the heavenly realms in Christ Jesus." – Ephesians 2:6. This was the case "for in Him we live and move and have our being." – Acts 17:28. What about the mother of the King of kings and Lord of lords? God mesmerised her with His graces and exalted her beyond description.

On the queenship of Mary, St. Alphonsus Ligouri writes: "Because the virgin Mary was raised to such a lofty dignity as to be the mother of the King of kings, it is deservedly and by every right that the Church has honoured her with the title of 'Queen'."[6]

Pope Pius XII elaborated further thus: "Now, in the accomplishing of this work of redemption, the Blessed Virgin Mary was most closely associated with Christ; and so, it is fitting to sing in the sacred liturgy: "Near the cross of Our Lord Jesus Christ there stood, sorrowful, the Blessed Mary, Queen of Heaven and Queen of the World." Hence, as the devout disciple of St. Anselm (Eadmer, ed.) wrote in the Middle Ages: "Just as . . . God, by making all through His power, is Father and Lord of all, so the blessed Mary, by repairing all through her merits, is Mother and Queen of all; for God is the Lord of all things, because by His command He establishes each of them in its own nature, and Mary is the Queen of all things, because she restores each to its original dignity through the grace which she merited. For "just as Christ, because He redeemed us, is our Lord and king by a special title, so the Blessed Virgin also (is our queen), on account of the unique manner in which she assisted in our redemption, by giving of her own substance, by freely offering Him for us, by her singular desire and petition for, and active interest in, our salvation."[7]

Whenever we are reflecting on the biblical revelations of Mary, we need always remember this revelation through apostle John: "And there are also many other things which

---

[6] Pius XII. "Ad Caeli Reginam (October 11, 1954) | PIUS XII." Www.vatican.va, 11 Oct. 1954, www.vatican.va/content/pius-xii/en/encyclicals/documents/hf_p-xii_enc_11101954_ad-caeli-reginam.html. para 25

[7] Ibid. — para 36 - 37

Jesus did, the which, if they should be written every one, I suppose that even the world itself could not contain the books that should be written." – John 21:25. If it is the case that the Spirit left us so much having revealed all that is essential for our salvation concerning Jesus Christ, His words and works, how much more about Mary? As the Secret Garden of the Most High, her privileges, graces, blessedness, exaltation, coronation and roles were hidden in the passages of the sacred scriptures.

Thoughts of the Pope and Early Church Writers on Lioness of Judah

In this chapter, I will simply echo the voice of the Holy Father, Pope Pius XII and other Patriarchs and Matriarchs of the Church on the excellency of the Mothe of the King of kings, Lord of lords, Jesus Christ, the Lion of the tribe of Judah. A close look at their writings regarding titles attributed to this Excellent Lady, we see the law of biogenesis in action. Mary is who she is as a result of the graces God lavished on her to become the Mother of His Son, Jesus Christ. Since I am letting them speak freely, I will simply mark their thoughts and prayers with quotation marks.

The Holy Father started by reminding us that "from the earliest ages of the catholic church a Christian people, whether in time of triumph or more especially in time of crisis, has addressed prayers of petition and hymns of praise and veneration to the Queen of Heaven. And never has that hope wavered which they placed in the Mother of the Divine King, Jesus Christ; nor has that faith ever failed by which we are taught that Mary, the Virgin Mother of God, reigns with a mother's solicitude over the entire world, just as she is crowned in heavenly blessedness with the glory of a Queen."

He then made it clear that regarding Our Blessed Mother, "We do not wish to propose a new truth to be believed by Christians, since the title and the arguments on which Mary's queenly dignity is based have already been clearly set forth, and are to be found in ancient documents of the Church and in the books of the sacred liturgy" and the Scriptures.

The purpose of reflecting on the person of Mary, the Holy Father stated is "that We may renew the praises of Our heavenly Mother, and enkindle a more fervent devotion towards her, to the spiritual benefit of all mankind". Para 7

The Church's Early Writers on Mary

"Hence it is not surprising that the early writers of the Church called Mary "the Mother of the King" and "the Mother of the Lord," basing their stand on the words of St. Gabriel the archangel, who foretold that the Son of Mary would reign forever, and on the words of Elizabeth who greeted her with reverence and called her "the Mother of my Lord." Thereby they clearly signified that she derived a certain eminence and exalted station from the royal dignity of her Son.

So it is that St. Ephrem, burning with poetic inspiration, represents her as speaking in this way: "Let Heaven sustain me in its embrace, because I am honoured above it. For heaven was not Thy mother, but Thou hast made it Thy throne. How much more honourable and venerable than the throne of a king is her mother." And in another place he thus prays to her: ". . . Majestic and Heavenly Maid, Lady, Queen, protect and keep me under your wing lest Satan the sower of destruction glory over me, lest my wicked foe be victorious against me."

St. Gregory Nazianzen calls Mary "the Mother of the King of the universe," and the "Virgin Mother who brought forth the King of the whole world," while Prudentius asserts that the Mother marvels "that she has brought forth God as man, and even as Supreme King."

And this royal dignity of the Blessed Virgin Mary is quite clearly indicated through direct assertion by those who call her "Lady," "Ruler" and "Queen."

In one of the homilies attributed to Origen, Elizabeth calls Mary "the Mother of my Lord." and even addresses her as "Thou, my Lady."[14]

The same thing is found in the writings of St. Jerome where he makes the following statement amidst various interpretations of Mary's name: "We should realize that Mary means Lady in the Syrian Language."[15] After him St. Chrysologus says the same thing more explicitly in these words: "The Hebrew word 'Mary' means 'Domina.' The Angel therefore addresses her as 'Lady' to preclude all servile fear in the Lord's Mother, who was born and was called 'Lady' by the authority and command of her own Son."

Moreover Epiphanius, the bishop of Constantinople, writing to the Sovereign Pontiff Hormisdas, says that we should pray that the unity of the Church may be preserved "by the grace of the holy and consubstantial Trinity and by the prayers of Mary, Our Lady, the holy and glorious Virgin and Mother of God."

The Blessed Virgin, sitting at the right hand of God to pray for us is hailed by another writer of that same era in these words, "the Queen of mortal man, the most holy Mother of God."

St. Andrew of Crete frequently attributes the dignity of a Queen to the Virgin Mary. For example, he writes, "Today He transports from her earthly dwelling, as Queen of the human race, His ever-Virgin Mother, from whose womb He, the living God, took on human form."

And in another place he speaks of "the Queen of the entire human race faithful to the exact meaning of her name, who is exalted above all things save only God himself."

Likewise St. Germanus speaks to the humble Virgin in these words: "Be enthroned, Lady, for it is fitting that you should sit in an exalted place since you are a Queen and glorious above all kings." He likewise calls her the "Queen of all of those who dwell on earth."

She is called by St. John Damascene "Queen, ruler, and lady," and also "the Queen of every creature." Another ancient writer of the Eastern Church calls her "favoured Queen," "the perpetual Queen beside the King, her son," whose "snow-white brow is crowned with a golden diadem."

And finally, St. Ildephonsus of Toledo gathers together almost all of her titles of honour in this salutation: "O my Lady, my Sovereign, You who rule over me, Mother of my Lord . . . Lady among handmaids, Queen among sisters."[8]

---

[8] Pius XII. "Ad Caeli Reginam (October 11, 1954) | PIUS XII." Www.vatican.va, 11 Oct. 1954, www.vatican.va/content/pius-xii/en/encyclicals/documents/hf_p-xii_enc_11101954_ad-caeli-reginam.html. para 1, 6, 7, 9-21

Exhortation – Wonderfully and Fearfully Made

Concerning you, no matter your state of birth, listen to God. Whatever the circumstance you are in right now, listen to God. Whatever has been said about you by your experiences, circumstances, flesh and blood, the world around you, and sciences, listen to God, believe and trust Him over and above all else. He made a revelation about you. Confess by your words and believe in your heart what He said concerning you as per Spirit's revelation: "For you created my inmost being; you knit me together in my mother's womb. I praise you because I am fearfully and wonderfully made; your works are wonderful; I know that full well. My frame was not hidden from you when I was made in the secret place when I was woven together in the depths of the earth. Your eyes saw my unformed body; all the days ordained for me were written in your book before one of them came to be. How precious to me are your thoughts, God! How vast is the sum of them! Were I to count them, they would outnumber the grains of sand —   when I awake, I am still with you." – Psalm 139:13-18.

Holy Spirit reveals that like the incarnation of Jesus Christ, God carefully planned your coming into the world before ever you were born. It was thus revealed: "Then God said, "Let us make mankind in our image, in our likeness, so that they may rule over the fish in the sea and the birds in the sky, over the livestock and all the wild animals, and over all the creatures that move along the ground." So, God created mankind in his own image, in the image of God he created them; male and female he created them." – Genesis 1:26-27. God has a plan for me. The first plan He has for you is to have dominion over other created things. Hence, God planned from the beginning that you live a life of dominion and victory. It is still his plan today for you. This is the reason we should not accept any other life that is short of God's intended plan for us. "For I know the plans I have for you," declares the Lord, "plans to prosper you and not to harm you, plans to give you hope and a future." – Jeremiah 29:11. Jesus Christ, the Lion of Judah, coming into the world through the Lioness of Judah with the purpose to restore us to the God's original plan for us said: "I have come that they may have life, and have it to the full." – John 10:10b. God, through Jesus Christ has made us become a partaker of His divine nature – 2 Peter 1:4. Jesus partook of our human nature through Virgin Mary that we may partake of His divine nature.

Jesus Christ while in the world said concerning you: "You are the light of [Christ to] the world. A city set on a hill cannot be hidden; nor does anyone light a lamp and put it under a basket, but on a lampstand, and it gives light to all who are in the house. Let your light shine before men in such a way that they may see your good deeds and moral excellence, and [recognise and honour and] glorify your Father who is in heaven." Matthew 5:14-16 (AMP).

You have been born again. You have been born of God. You have confessed with your mouth that Jesus Christ is your Lord and personal Saviour and personal Friend, and you have believed in your heart. Hence, the scripture revealed this concerning you: "Whoever confesses and acknowledges that Jesus is the Son of God, God abides in him, and he in God. We have come to know [by personal observation and experience], and have believed [with deep, consistent faith] the love which God has for us. God is love, and the one who abides in love abides in God, and God abides continually in him. In this [union and fellowship with Him], love is completed and perfected with us, so that we may have confidence in the day of judgment [with assurance and boldness to face Him]; **because as He is, so are we in this world.** – 1 John 4:15-17 (emphasis is mine).

The Spirit said regarding Jesus Christ: "He was in the world, and though the world was made through him, the world did not recognize him. He came to that which was his own, but his own did not receive him." – John 1:10-11. It is then not surprising that you do not know yourself, who you truly are and those around you do not know neither. Receive and believe God about you and His revelation of you. You are truly fearfully and wonderfully made. You have received Jesus, and the Spirit says about you: "Yet to all who did receive him, to those who believed in his name, he gave the right to become children of God, children born not of natural descent, nor of human decision or a husband's will, but born of God." – John 1:12-13. You can see that it is not only that you are wonderfully and fearfully made but you are now rightfully a child of God. "Flesh gives birth to flesh, but the Spirit gives birth to spirit." – John 3:6. Hence, the Lion of Judah can only be given birth to by a Lioness of Judah. If you are a child of God, which you are, you should now recognise who you truly are in this world, a spirit, like your Father who is the Spirit, but still dwelling in a body.

This Spirit of truth that gave birth to you, "The world cannot accept him, because it neither sees him nor knows him. But you know him, for he lives with you and will be in you (at this time the Spirit had not yet come)." – John 3:6. It is the same reason that the world cannot accept and acknowledge the Spirit that they cannot accept and acknowledge who you are. Do not join the world in doubting yourself, your identity and your capabilities. You should know and acknowledge who you are in God and for God.

How To Pray the Rosary

Praying the Rosary
1. While holding the crucifix, make the Sign of the Cross and say the Apostles' Creed.
2. On the first bead and other single beads, pray Our Father...
3. Pray three Hail Marys on the following three beads for an increase in faith, hope, charity and intentions of the Holy Father.
4. Pray the Glory Be ...
5. Announce the mystery, imagine the event, and meditate on it by itself or in association with whatever the mystery brings to your heart.
6. On the single bead pray Our Father ...
7. Pray the Hail Mary ... on the ten beads while meditating on the first mystery. (Repeat nos 4 and 5)
8. Pray on the single bead the Our Father ...
9. Pray on the ten beads Hail Mary ...
10. Repeat as in numbers 4 and 5 until the last decade (i.e. ten beads)
11. After the last decade you can pray the Hail Holy Queen...

The Sign of the Cross
In the name of the Father, and of the Son, and of the Holy Spirit. Amen.

The Apostles' Creed

I believe in God, the Father almighty, Creator of heaven and earth. and in Jesus Christ, his only Son, our Lord, who was conceived by the Holy Spirit, born of the Virgin Mary, suffered under Pontius Pilate, was crucified, died, and was buried; he descended into hell; on the third day he rose again from the dead; he ascended into heaven, and is seated at the right hand of God the Father almighty; from there he will come to judge the living and the dead.

I believe in the Holy Spirit, the holy catholic Church, the communion of saints, the forgiveness of sins, the resurrection of the body, and life everlasting. Amen.

The Lord's Prayer (Our Father)

Our Father, who art in heaven, hallowed be thy name; thy kingdom come; thy will be done on earth as it is in heaven. Give us this day our daily bread; and forgive us our trespasses as we forgive those who trespass against us; and lead us not into temptation, but deliver us from evil. Amen.

Hail Mary

Hail Mary, full of grace. The Lord is with thee. Blessed art thou among women, and blessed is the fruit of thy womb, Jesus.

Holy Mary, Mother of God, pray for us sinners, now and at the hour of our death. Amen.

The Glory Be (The Doxology)

Glory be to the Father, and to the Son, and to the Holy Spirit.

As it was in the beginning, is now, and ever shall be, world without end. Amen.

Fatima Invocation
O my Jesus, forgive us our sins, save us from the fires of hell, and lead all souls to heaven, especially those most in need of thy mercy.

The Joyful Mysteries
(Mondays and Saturdays)
1. The Annunciation of the birth of the Lord to Mary by the archangel
Gabriel (Lk 1:26-38).
2. The Visitation of Our Lady with St. Elizabeth, the mother of St. John the
Baptist (Lk 1:39-56).
3. The Nativity of Our Lord (Mt 1:18-25; Lk 2:1-20).
4. The Presentation of the Christ Child in the Temple (Lk 2:22-32).
5. The Finding of the Child Jesus in the Temple (Lk 2:41-52).

The Sorrowful Mysteries
(Tuesdays and Fridays)
1. The Agony in the Garden of Gethsemane (Mk 14:32-42).
2. The Scourging of Jesus (Jn 19:1).
3. The Crowning with Thorns (Mk 15:16-20).
4. The Carrying of the Cross (Jn 19:12-17).
5. The Crucifixion (Mt 27:33-56; Mk 15:22-41; Lk 23:26-49; Jn 19:16-30).

The Luminous Mysteries
(Thursdays)
1. The Baptism of Our Lord in the River Jordan (Mt 3:13-16).
2. The Self-Manifestation of Our Lord at the Wedding at Cana (Jn 2:1-11).

3. The Proclamation of the Kingdom of God (Mk 1:14-15).
4. The Transfiguration of Our Lord (Mt 17:1-8; Lk 9:28-29).
5. The Last Supper, when the Eucharist was Instituted (Mt 26).

The Glorious Mysteries
(Wednesdays and Sundays)
1. The Resurrection (Lk 24:1-12; Jn 20).
2. The Ascension (Lk 24:50-53; Acts 1:1-12).
3. The Descent of the Holy Spirit at Pentecost (Acts 2:1-4).
4. The Assumption of the Blessed Virgin Mary (Song 2:8-14).
5. The Coronation of the Blessed Mother (Rev 12:1-4).

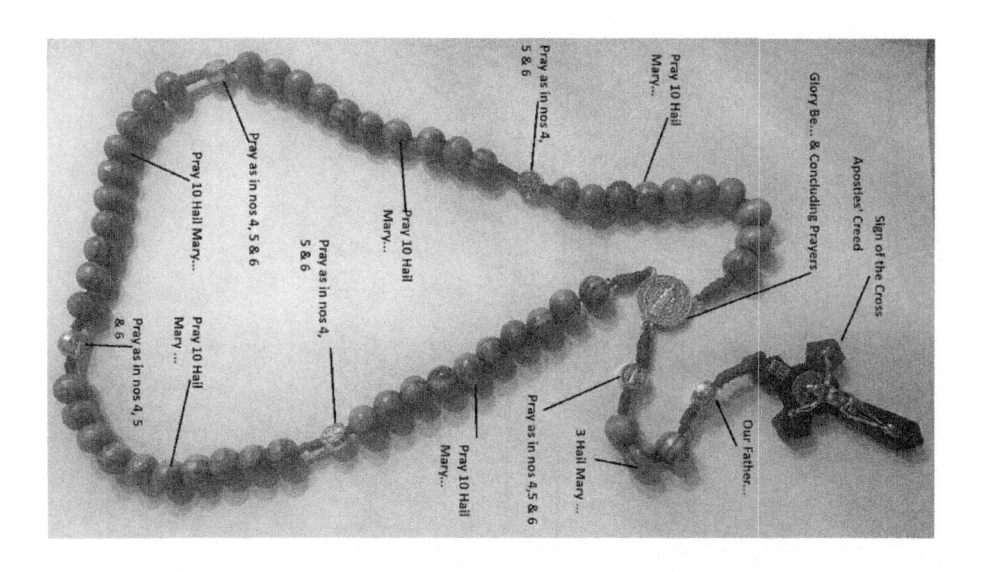

Printed in Great Britain
by Amazon